The BIG Metric Ninja Foodi Cookbook

DAVID SMALL

COPYRIGHT © 2021 DAVID SMALL

www.handyinthekitchen.com

ISBN: 9798706849689   (Hardback Colour version)

ISBN: 9798700611503   (Paperback Black & White version)

ISBN: 9798599644248   (Paperback Colour version)

DEDICATION

I'd like to take the opportunity to thank my Mother, Hilary for teaching me to cook all the necessary meals growing up so that I could fend for myself, enjoy working in the kitchen and most importantly, feed my kids. There are more than a fair few recipes from her in this book, including scones, bundt marble cake and the carrot cake.

I'd also like to thank my two favourite people in the world, Emily & Liam, for their patience with my various cooking experiments as well as their brutal honesty when rating the meals that I have cooked for them!

Finally, a big thanks to SharkNinja, for making such a versatile device that takes <u>so</u> much of the stress out of cooking

CONTENTS

DESSERT RECIPES 135

SOUP RECIPES 145

CONVERSION TABLES 159

ADDITIONAL SAUCES/DIPS & STUFFING 161

INDEX OF INGREDIENTS 165

INTRODUCTION TO THE NINJA FOODI

So you 've taken the plunge, you've bought a Ninja Foodi, no doubt unpacked it and now you're ready to get started.

There are endless creations awaiting you now but first you should discover what all the various functions are, what they do and why the hell are there two lids with this thing?

STICKY BEEF & BROCCOLI

I love my Nina Foodi.

Yes, that's quite a bold statement and maybe I am exaggerating somewhat but I do have very strong feelings for it.

I remember struggling to sleep one night, zapping through TV channels in the hope to find something mundane to watch that I could fall asleep to. I forget which channel it was, it doesn't really matter, but one of those rolling infomercials started to play out, introducing the Ninja Foodi.

I didn't really pay too much attention at first until the presenter showed a perfectly cooked roast chicken, cooked in less than an hour, crispy skin, fall-off-the-bone meat, the works. It spiked my attention and before long I was glued to the presentation.

I've definitely got to get one of those. A quick reach over to my phone, found the app for the store named after the world's largest river, and bingo, ordered.

A few days later I collected my new best friend from the post office, unpacked it, found a space for it in the corner of my kitchen and grinned. "Now what?", I thought to myself.

As many first time Foodi owners will know, the uncertainty or sheer bewilderment of what to actually do with the thing, how to prepare the food that goes into it, how long it takes to cook and so many other questions are the first hurdles to clear before going ahead and using it confidently.

Sure, there's a booklet that accompanies the device and to be honest, none of the recipes inside that booklet jumped out at me so it was time to go online for help.

You will notice that I will explain many details of how exactly to perform certain tasks within the first few recipes, perhaps these are overly obvious to you the reader or tiresome even, if you have been using your Foodi for a while already.

So please do not panic, the extreme level of detail will decrease as the book goes on, down to just the ingredients, method and occasional extra tip after each recipe title.

Every now-and-then a big black box will appear, like the one below this statement. This is for me to explain something that is often asked in the various online forums and social media websites that is important, yet doesn't really go-with-the-flow of the book.

I have "insert-name-of-food" that takes "insert-time" at "insert-temperature" in my oven. How long would this take using the BAKE/ROAST function in the Foodi?

I see this question asked so many times in posts on the various forums.

The answer that I usually give is to take the time as instructed, reduce by 20%, and reduce the cooking temperature by 10°C.

WHAT CAN MY FOODI DO?

Figure 1: The Foodi display and button panel

The first thing to notice about your Ninja Foodi is that it has two lids. One lid is attached and one is not. The pressure lid, or as I refer to it, the other lid, is completely detachable and sits quite innocently in my saucepan drawer in my kitchen, out-of-the-way. Terms in this book in CAPITAL letters refer to the button on the front of the Foodi display and button panel. The model I use has a display panel that looks as shown above.

HOW IS EACH LID USED?

The crisping or built-in lid (as I will refer to it in this book) is the hardest to clean part of the device, sadly, and quite possibly the part of the device that I'd love to be able to clean after every single use.

The built-in lid, known as the crisping lid is a fair bit more

technical than the pressure lid as it contains an electronic heating filament, a fan as various more pieces of sorcery that will only bore both of us.

WHAT CAN I DO WITH THE PRESSURE LID?

Figure 2: How to install and remove the pressure cooker lid. Look for the triangle marks on the front of the Foodi and align it with the same triangle mark on the pressure cooker lid, as shown below.

Pressure cook – Basically liquid is added to the base of the cooking pot, it is heated rapidly to create steam. This steam cannot escape from the device, thus building up pressure.

Under pressure, this steam infuses moisture into what is

being cooked.

Due to the extreme pressure, ingredients are cooked considerably faster than at normal room conditions and are cooked from the centre outwards. Pressure cooking requires that the vent on the lid is turned to SEAL rather than VENT. This stops water moisture from escaping the device and thus allows the build-up of pressure.

When pressure cooking has completed, a release of pressure is required. Releasing the pressure can be a little intimidating to people who are new to pressure cooking - especially the quick release with the noise and jet of steam.

The two distinct and separate ways of releasing pressure have different effects upon the ingredients and the environment in your kitchen.

Figure 3: The pressure cooker lid showing the vent switched to the VENT position. The float valve is pictured to the right of the vent dial, shown here in the fully depressed position

Natural or slow release – no action is taken. The countdown timer simply reaches the zero mark and starts counting upwards for convenience. When a recipe states "Natural release for five minutes", simply let the pressure-cooking countdown reach zero with the vent pointing to the SEAL mark and then allow the Foodi to count up to five minutes. Implied is also a quick release after that which

means switching the vent to the VENT position until all pressure has been released.

You will know when pressure has been released when the lid is able to be removed without any effort required.

A natural release is a bit anticlimactic in comparison to a quick pressure release. There is no jet of steam when the natural pressure release starts. You don't want to open the valve quickly when the ingredients inside could be foaming. You will get foam shooting out through the vent, so use a natural pressure release when cooking oats, soup or pasta. You will also want to use a natural release for large cuts of meat.

Just like you'd let meat rest after grilling it, a slow natural release is said to let the meat relax and be more tender, less coarse or stringy.

Quick release – simply switching the vent from the SEAL position to the VENT position. A fast release of steam from the device will take place. Be careful not to burn your hands or face when using this method. Steam can over time cause formation of mold in colder areas, such as corners of the ceiling and window areas, so it is highly recommended to either open windows for ventilation during this procedure or turning on an extractor fan. Also be careful with low-hanging cupboards as these are usually wooden and will easily absorb moisture when bombarded with steam. Persistent use under such cupboards will result in swollen, damaged cupboards as well as steam-filled enclosures.

Some Ninja Foodi devices are fitted with a red button (known as a float valve) next to the vent dial on the pressure lid, others have a silver button.

A recipe that takes an hour to cook in the oven, would need only 20 minutes in the Ninja Foodi as a pressure cooker

Truth is, these buttons are identical and have two purposes.

Firstly, the float valve rises as pressure builds within the device, being fully raised as pressure is reached. The float valve will fall to its lowest level as pressure is fully released.

The second use of the float valve is to quickly release all pressure if depressed. This is for emergency use only and is not a recommended method for releasing pressure, partly due to the extreme speed at which steam is released and due to the fact that the steam is not filtered, so both water and fat is spurted out with gusto! The reverse side of the venting seal has a filter to hinder fat from being spurted-out into the open air.

Figure 4: Vent dial

Using a quick release stops the pressure-cooking really quickly. Therefore, one should only use a quick pressure release when cooking ingredients, such as vegetables, that you want to avoid over-cooking and spoiling.

Some recipes for other one-pot cooking devices may refer to performing an "**Intermittent release**". While this type of pressure release is rare when it comes to recipes, it is possible to perform on the Ninja Foodi.

It is a convenient way to quickly release pressure for foods such as pastas, soups, and certain grains, which are prone to foaming or spitting if you try to release pressure with a quick release but would be over-cooked with a natural pressure release.

With this method, you simply switch the vent from SEAL to VENT and back to SEAL in short intervals. This allows the pressure to escape more quickly than a natural pressure release and also prevents foam from coming out of the vent.

With some foods, one or two closed intervals is all I need before I can leave the vent dial in the VENT; with other foods, if the foaming is particularly bad, I will close the vent and wait a minute or two, then slide the vent to VENT again and continue opening and closing the vent as required.

Steam – The STEAM method of cooking requires a fair amount of liquid to be added to the cooking pot and the vent being set to the VENT position. Unlike the pressure-cooking method, steam does not cook under pressure as steam is released through the vent dial.

Figure 5: Steaming rack

Steam infuses moisture into the ingredients, allowing for flavours to be sealed-in while maintaining the texture of the food.

Due to the amount of moisture generated by this method of cooking, situate the Foodi close to an open window or extractor fan.

Keep away from low-hanging cupboards to avoid permanent damage to kitchen cupboards.

Steaming food usually requires the use of the metal steaming rack that was supplied with your Ninja Foodi. This ensures that the ingredients are kept out of the layer of liquid sitting at the base of the cooking pot.

Note: A lot of steam comes from the Foodi unit when using the Steam function, and this is completely normal. Leave the pressure release valve in the VENT position for Steam, Slow Cook, and Sear/Sauté.

If you place your Ninja Foodi underneath an extractor fan hood, make sure that if it sits on a hob, the surface is not still warm from cooking. The base of the Foodi is plastic and will melt very quickly if placed on a hot surface.

If the Foodi must be placed onto a hot surface due to space limitations, make sure that you have an isolating block, a thick chopping-board or another insulated surface between the Foodi and the source of the heat.

Slow cook – Cook your food at a lower temperature for longer periods of time using the SLOW COOK button.

The Slow Cook HIGH setting may be adjusted anywhere between 4 and 12 hours; the Slow Cook LOW setting may be adjusted anywhere between 6 and 12 hours.

Sear / Sauté - To use the unit for browning meats, sautéing vegetables, simmering sauces, and more using the SEAR / SAUTÉ button.

You can use this function with either the crisping lid in the open position or the pressure lid with the pressure release vent valve in the VENT position.

WHAT CAN I DO WITH THE CRISPING / BUILT-IN LID?

Air crisp – To use the unit as an air-crisper to give foods crispiness and crunch with little to no oil, select the AIR CRISP button.

NinjaKitchen™ recommend that the supplied air crisp basket be used when air crisping. Do not remove the detachable diffuser from the base of the basket for cooking. This enables fan-assisted hot air to be forced down from the heating filament, across the food, through the base of the basket and then diverted upwards at a different angle, due to its propeller-like shape and form.

Do not use spray oils, such as Frylite™, to coat your food before air crisping. This type of oil when heated to its smoke point can easily remove the non-stick coating of the air crisp basket.

(The smoke point of oil is the temperature at which it stops shimmering and starts smoking. The smoke point is also called the burning point of oil and each oil type has its own specific smoke point).

If you take the steaming rack in its upside-down position as shown to the left, then pull the legs outwards, it functions as a convenient tool to remove the hot air crisp basket from the Foodi without burning your hands. It's very difficult to describe the action in writing. Perhaps the following photographs will better explain how this feature works.

Bake / Roast – To use the unit as an oven for tender meats, baked treats, bread and more, select the BAKE / ROAST button. Even though this is effectively a comparable device to your kitchen oven, due to its size and the effectiveness of the built-in fan, the bake function cooks food faster than in a regular oven. If your recipe tells you to cook at X°C for Y minutes, reduce by the time Y by 20%, and reduce the cooking temperature X by 10°C.

For example, cook at 200°C for 30 minutes in a regular oven, then you would bake in the Foodi for 24 minutes at 190°C. This is simply my rule-of-thumb and not official advice from NinjaKitchen™, but from my experience this rule-of-thumb seems to work well.

You can use any of the supplied accessories to bake, be it the air crisp basket or the steaming rack, it really does not matter too much.

I regularly cook part-baked bread-rolls using the steaming rack and the bake function. Bread-rolls that are labelled as requiring ten minutes in a regular oven take just six minutes at 180°C and do not require turning during cooking.

Grill – Use the GRILL setting to caramelise and brown-off your food. For consistent browning, make sure the ingredients are arranged in an even layer with no overlapping. If ingredients are overlapping, make sure to shake half way through the set cooking time.

*Figure 6: Use the steaming rack to aid easy removal of the hot air crisp basket from the cooking pot. After aligning the divets of the steaming rack into the handles of the air crisp basket, then lifting up the legs of the rack, the air crisp basket is tightly clamped for safe and easy removal. **This does not work with the 9-in-1 Foodi***

EITHER LID

Keep Warm – After pressure cooking, steaming, or slow cooking, the unit will automatically switch to Keep Warm mode and start counting up. Keep Warm will stay on for 12 hours, or you may press KEEP WARM to turn it off. Keep Warm mode is not intended to heat food from cold, but to keep pressure-cooked food at a food-safe temperature.

Standby - The POWER button turns off the unit and stops all cooking. After 10 minutes with no interaction with the control panel, the unit will enter standby mode, hence no power to the unit.

THE RECIPES IN THIS BOOK

As you thumb through this book, you will no doubt notice that the recipes vary in length and depth, and for very good reason.

Writing the recipes, I assume that you are familiar with how the Ninja Foodi operates so I have intentionally only included the in-depth instructions in the beginner recipes section that follows.

Thereafter the assumption is made that you know how not to burn or scald yourselves, you know that you shouldn't use metal implements with the cooking pot and the difference between quick release and natural release when it comes to using the pressure cooker function.

Also, you will notice a little box next to the ingredients list.

This is intended just as a quick guide as to roughly how long each recipe should take to prepare and then cook. Also is how much skill is required for anyone attempting the recipe, some of us are more confident in the kitchen than others.

Serves	2
Difficulty	●●○
Functions	Sear/Sauté Pressure Bake/Roast
Time Prep	5
Time Cook	30

The "serves" entry is also just a guide, as obviously everyone eats different amount of food, depending on age and size, I guess. When you see the words "Pressure" or "Steam" appear in the functions list, grab your pressure lid and keep it handy, you'll need it.

I should also issue a little apology for the photographs of the food that I have cooked.

I'm not an expert photographer but armed with my iPhone, I was able to take some pictures that demonstrate how the food looks when it is cooked based on following the instructions that I lay out.

Finally, it's worth adding that while your Foodi will live for most of its life, tucked-away somewhere in the corner of the worktop in your kitchen, when you and your family enjoy a caravanning holiday, don't forget the Ninja.

It's the perfect device to take with you due to its versatility.

There's nothing worse than trying to cook for a family of four with just two hob rings and a kettle, trust me… and take this book with you!

BEGINNER RECIPES

We will start off with simple things to cook.

I will explain how to cook these simple things in minute detail, just in case you are new to the Foodi and feel somewhat baffled by some of the terms used in the standard recipes.

JACKET POTATO

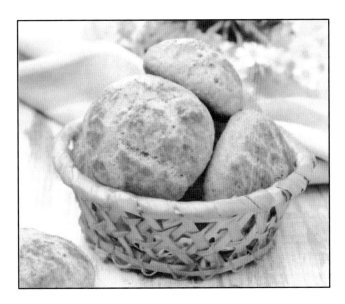

1. Pre-heat the oven to 200°C

2. Wet under the tap with a splash of cold water

3. Carefully place onto the oven shelf without making any mess (especially if the bread rolls have seeds on them)

4. Bake for 15 minutes, rotating half way through to ensure evenness of baking.

5. Carefully remove from the oven so to avoid further mess

6. Carefully slice them open as the make one hell of a mess due to them being too crispy

Well, now I have my Ninja Foodi, so this is my current method.

PART-BAKED BREAD ROLLS Ⓥ

Now that I have my Foodi sitting proud in the corner of my kitchen, I don't need to buy fresh bread rolls quite as regularly as I did before I got the Foodi.

Serves	1-6
Difficulty	ooo
Functions	**Bake**
Time Prep	0
Time Cook	7

I buy part-baked bread rolls from the supermarket in packs of 8 or 10. I have bought these bread rolls before I had the Foodi but they are definitely more convenient now.

Why?

Well, if I were to put four of these bread rolls in the oven to bake, I would need to do the following.

NINJA FOODI METHOD:

1. Open the Foodi, remove the accessories and turn on. Select BAKE/ROAST for 7 minutes at 180°C

2. Put 2, 3, 4, 5 or even 6 bread rolls onto the up-turned steaming rack. Close the lid. Press Start/Stop.

That's it. Done. There's no mess created other than one or two slight crumbs if they are packed too close together, they are moister when eating and slicing open, they take less time, they taste more like they would coming straight from a bakery, they need no maintenance/turning during baking… and so on.

To me that is a no-brainer! So, I make sure now that I have several different types of part-baked bread rolls in my bread-bin, sealed securely but ready to bake at a moment's notice.

STEAKHOUSE CHIPS Ⓥ

Firstly, decide if you are going to cook the chips with or without the potato skin. In terms of timing, it really makes no difference.

Serves	3-5
Difficulty	ооо
Functions	**Air crisp**
Time Prep	5
Time Cook	25

Personally, I prefer them with the skin on but of course, if you use a large potato, then the chips from the centre of the potato will not have skin on, other than on the ends perhaps. Source sweet and starchy potatoes for the best results, look for King Edward, Maris Piper, Romano, Désirée, or russet potatoes and you won't go far wrong. Avoid waxy potatoes, a category that includes any with red skin, new potatoes, and fingerling potatoes.

What I like to do is cut each potato in half, then quarters. Then cut the quarter slices into half, and repeat until they are sliced into around 1 cm thick slices, thicker if you'd like.

The Daily Mirror reports that scientists have found that soaking potatoes reduces amounts of acrylamide, a chemical that is formed "when starch-rich foods are cooked at high temperatures". Apparently, two hours of soaking reduces levels by 48%, half an hour by 38% and just washing them lowers levels by 23%.

There is evidence of a link between acrylamide and cancer in rats, though evidence for the link in humans is limited and it is classified as a "potential human carcinogen". Until further research better establishes whether or not acrylamide does cause cancer in humans, it seems sensible to consider limiting consumption of it where possible. Why tell you all this? Well, another benefit to soaking potatoes is that the resultant chip or fry will be much crispier on the outside yet soft and fluffy on the inside.

So, if time permits, soak the cut chips in cold tap water for up to two hours. Thank me later.

INGREDIENTS

- 400g - 600g potatoes cut into chip shapes
- 1 dessert spoon full of sunflower oil
- Salt & Additional seasoning (optional)

METHOD

1. Cut the potatoes into chip shapes, soak, then put them into a deep plate or bowl. Add the dessert spoon of sunflower or other vegetable oil (but not olive oil).

2. Grind some sea salt or add a sprinkle of table salt. Optionally use a seasoning to beef-up the chips. I have tried to great success each of the following:

   - Paprika & salt
   - Garlic granules
   - Nando's peri-peri salt
   - Wedges salt – which contains paprika, salt, onion, pepper & chili… Or just use salt

3. Mix well with a spoon until every chip is coated lightly in oil & ideally salt. Tip. Put the air crisp basket into the foodi cooking pot. Tip the chips into the air crisp basket, letting any oil left in the bowl drip onto the top of the chips.

4. Close the built-in lid and AIR CRISP at 190°C for 25 minutes. You can open this lid without worrying about changing any timing or settings.

5. Open after ten minutes have elapsed to spoon stir the chips, close the lid and wait until finished. Sometimes, if I am cooking more than for three people, a better shake is required to get the chips cooked more even. Simply take out the basket, put a plate over it and shake vigorously over a sink.

TIPS

You can add a dessert spoon full of corn flour when tossing the chips in oil to make them extra crispy. For lower fat consumption, tip the air crisp basket contents onto kitchen paper and dab carefully to remove any excess oil before serving.

REHEATING PIZZA

INGREDIENTS

▪ Pizza slice

Serves	-
Difficulty	ooo
Functions	**Air crisp**
Time Prep	0
Time Cook	7

METHOD

1. Place the pizza slice into the air crisp basket. Select AIR CRISP and cook for 7 minutes at 160°C.

CRISPY POTATO SKINS Ⓥ

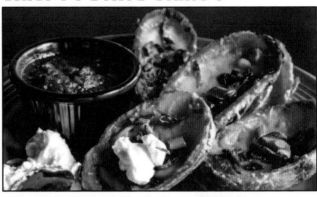

INGREDIENTS

▪ Potato skins

▪ Rapeseed oil

▪ Sea salt

▪ Ground paprika

Serves	-
Difficulty	ooo
Functions	**Air crisp**
Time Prep	1
Time Cook	7

METHOD

1. Don't throw away your potato peelings, simply wash them, dry them well and spray them in a bowl with rapeseed oil.

2. Add ground sea salt and dust them with ground paprika. Open the Foodi lid, insert the air crisp basket. Tip in the potato skins and close the lid. Select AIR CRISP and cook at 210°C for 7 minutes. Check after 6 minutes that they are not burning. Serve with a salsa or guacamole dip (*Recipe at the end of this book*), cream cheese & chives or melt cheese and sprinkle with bacon lardons. Enjoy.

FROZEN CHIPS ⓥ

INGREDIENTS

▪ Frozen chips

Serves	1-5
Difficulty	ooo
Functions	**Air crisp**
Time Prep	**0**
Time Cook	**18**

METHOD

1. Measure onto plates how many frozen chips are required. Place the air crisp basket into the cooking pot. Add the chips to the air crisp basket.

2. Select AIR CRISP, choose 180°C and cook for 18 minutes. After 9 minutes, open the lid quickly, stir the chips with a wooden spoon so that all chips at the bottom of the basket are now higher up and vice versa. Close the lid and continue to cook. After the 18 minutes cooking time, check that the chips are completely cooked through and add additional minutes if need be.

TIPS

Crinkle-cut frozen chips make for the crunchiest chip. For frozen steakhouse chips, I find that an additional 2 minutes using the BAKE/ROAST function before starting the AIR CRISP ensures that the centre of the chips are fluffy.

HARD-BOILED EGGS ⓥ

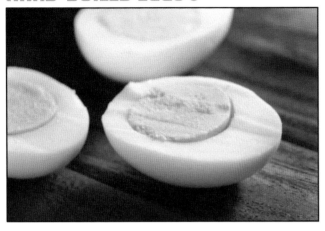

INGREDIENTS

- Up to 6 eggs
- 350ml of water

Serves	1-6
Difficulty	ooo
Functions	**Pressure**
Time Prep	0
Time Cook	9

METHOD

1. Place the steaming rack into the cooking pot, lowest side at the bottom. Place up to 7 eggs on the rack and pour 350ml of water into the base of the cooking pot. Install the pressure lid, set the vent to SEAL and select PRESSURE from the front display. Cook for 7 minutes using the high pressure setting.

2. After the timer has reached zero, switch the vent to VENT to quick release the pressure. Remove the eggs and place them into a bowl of cold water. To remove the egg shell, simply tap them onto your counter top and carefully remove the shell from all the boiled eggs.

SOFT-BOILED EGGS ⓥ

INGREDIENTS

- 2 medium-sized eggs

Serves	2-7
Difficulty	ooo
Functions	**Air crisp**
Time Prep	0
Time Cook	7-9

METHOD

1. Take two or more medium-sized eggs not straight from the refrigerator, let them get to room temperature.

2. If your eggs are stored in the refrigerator, increase the cooking time by two minutes. Preheat the Foodi by closing the lid, set BAKE/ROAST for one minute

3. Place two eggs onto the wire rack OR into the air crisp basket. Select AIR CRISP at the default 200 °C and cook for 7 minutes.

4. With the timing above, the eggs will contain runny yolks but cooked. Increase the time for hard-boiled eggs

JACKET POTATOES ⓥ

INGREDIENTS

- 2 (or more) Large potatoes
- 1 ½ dessert spoons of olive oil
- Sea salt
- A filling of your choice, for example:
    - Baked beans
    - Butter & salt
    - Spicy mayo (*recipe at the back of this book*)

Serves	1-4
Difficulty	●○○
Functions	**Pressure Bake/Roast Air crisp**
Time Prep	**1+**
Time Cook	**45**

- Grated cheese & salt
- Crème fraiche & bacon lardons
- Tuna, sweetcorn & mayonnaise, mixed
- Philadelphia soft cheese, topped with chives
- Spring onions, melted cheese & salad cream
- … and so on. Everyone has their own preferred personal jacket potato filling!

METHOD

1. Add 250ml of water in the cooking pot of the Ninja Foodi Take two (or more) large potatoes, wash them and prick them each twice with a fork.

15

2. Either using the wire rack or air crisp basket, place the potatoes into the Foodi. Place the pressure cooker lid onto the Foodi and turn the vent to the SEAL position

3. Select PRESSURE to pressure cook on the default high setting for 14 minutes. Note that it takes several minutes to achieve high pressure before the countdown starts.

4. After the countdown reaches zero allow the counter to count up 10 minutes before switching the vent from SEAL to VENT, to quick release the pressure from the Foodi.

5. Oil the potatoes with the olive oil and completely coat each potato fully. Be careful as the potatoes are very hot at this stage and oil transmits heat very easily.

6. Use a pastry brush or roll the potatoes in a bowl if you can. Salt lightly the outside of the potato skin. Empty the water from the Foodi and place the potatoes into the air crisp basket.

7. Select AIR CRISP and cook for 15 minutes at 200°C, checking in the last 2 minutes that they are not burning.

JACKET POTATO LOADED WITH BAKED BEANS

MAIN COURSE COMPONENTS & FULL RECIPES

This may be a weird title to some but the clarification is needed. Some of these recipes are complete, full meals whereas others are just parts of the main meal, a side dish is required to fill the plate.

CHEESE BURGER WITH WEDGES

EGG-FRIED-RICE Ⓥ

INGREDIENTS

- 350g American long-grain white rice (or equivalent)
- 700ml of boiling water
- 2 eggs
- 1 vegetable stock cube
- 2 dessert spoons of soy sauce
- ½ a teaspoon of five spice (Chinese-style mixed spice)
- 100g frozen or fresh peas
- 50g frozen or canned sweetcorn (drained)
- 1 small carrot, peeled and diced
- 2 small or 1 large spring onion, cut into fine rings
- 1 ½ dessert spoons of sesame oil

Serves	4
Difficulty	●○○
Functions	**Pressure Sear/Sauté**
Time Prep	**3**
Time Cook	**15**

METHOD

1. In a measuring jug, add 700ml of boiling water to a vegetable stock cube. Mix well.

2. Remove the air crisp basket from the Foodi and add the rice, five spice and vegetable stock to the cooking pot. Stir with a wooden or silicone spoon. Fit the pressure cooker lid and slide the vent to the SEAL position. Press PRESSURE on the display panel and cook on the default high setting for 4 minutes. Due to the amount of liquid in the cooker it may take up to 5 minutes to reach the desired pressure.

3. Peel and dice the carrot into ½ cm cubes or use the largest hole on a grater to roughly grate it. If you are using canned sweetcorn, open and drain the sweetcorn.

4. Remove the end of the spring onion, wash and cut from bottom to top the spring onions into fine rings.

5. After the countdown has reached zero, the natural release procedure will commence. Let the counter reach 2 minutes before switching the vent of the pressure cooker lid to the VENT position to start the quick release. After quick release has finished, the lid is easily removed.

6. Add the peas, carrot, spring onion rings and sweetcorn to the cooking pot.

7. Mix well and select SEAR/SAUTÉ, cook for a minute or so on the high setting. Using a wooden spoon, create a dip or a well in the centre of the rice. Measure the sesame oil into the well of rice.

8. Whisk 2 eggs with a fork or silicone spoon in a bowl and add to the rice well. Let the egg thicken, slowly cooking. After the egg mixture has cooked, add the soy sauce and stir-in to the rice using a wooden spoon until everything is mixed well. Turn off the Foodi and serve the rice.

SPINACH & BACON OMELETTE

INGREDIENTS

- 8 Eggs
- Butter
- ½ a bag of Baby spinach (100g)
- 6-10 rashers of Bacon
- Salt & Pepper
- 2 tablespoons of dried or chopped fresh Chives

Serves	4
Difficulty	●○○
Functions	**Bake/Roast**
Time Prep	**1**
Time Cook	**25**

METHOD

1. Chop the bacon. Select BAKE/ROAST at 200°C for 3 minutes to pre-heat. Grease a cake tin thoroughly with butter, leaving no part un-greased.

2. In a bowl, whisk all 8 eggs then add the spinach, salt, pepper and the chives. Pour the mixture into the cake tin. Throw in the chopped bacon.

3. Place the cake tin into the empty cooking pot. Select BAKE/ROAST and cook at 200°C for 20 minutes.

4. Serve and enjoy.

FROZEN CHICKEN BREAST FILLETS

INGREDIENTS

- 2 Chicken breast fillets (boneless, frozen, between 180 to 250g in weight)
- Olive oil
- Cracked black pepper
- Sea salt

Serves	2
Difficulty	●○○
Functions	**Pressure Grill**
Time Prep	**1**
Time Cook	**23**

METHOD

1. Place the chicken breasts on the steaming rack with the surface of the rack closest to the top of the Foodi. Add 250ml of water to the base of the cooking pot.

2. Fit the pressure lid and switch the vent dial to SEAL. Select PRESSURE. Pressure cook on the high setting for 10 minutes.

3. Quick release pressure by switching the vent dial to VENT. When pressure has been fully released, remove the pressure lid. Brush the chicken lightly with olive oil. Season with sea salt and cracked black pepper. Close the built-in lid and select GRILL. Cook for 10 minutes, checking for burning after 8 minutes.

4. Serve and enjoy.

SWEET CHILI CHICKEN BREAST

INGREDIENTS

- 4 Chicken breast fillets (boneless, fresh, between 170 to 225g each in weight)
- Olive oil
- Sweet chili sauce
- Sea salt

Serves	4
Difficulty	●○○
Functions	**Pressure** **Grill**
Time Prep	2
Time Cook	21

METHOD

1. Place the chicken breasts on the steaming rack with the surface of the rack closest to the top of the Foodi. Add 250ml of water to the base of the cooking pot.

2. Fit the pressure lid and switch the vent dial to SEAL. Select PRESSURE. Pressure cook on the high setting for 8 minutes.

3. Quick release pressure by switching the vent dial to VENT. When pressure has been fully released, remove the pressure lid.

4. Brush the chicken lightly with olive oil. Season with sea salt and brush with sweet chili sauce.

5. Close the built-in lid and select GRILL. Cook for 10 minutes, checking for burning after 8 minutes.

6. Serve and enjoy.

CHEATERS SAUSAGE ROLLS

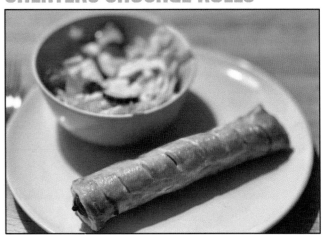

This recipe is a particular favourite of my little ones. It's more a snack than a full meal. British and Irish Pork sausages tend to stay very hot after cooking and have a huge fat content. Bratwurst sausages (Aldi, Lidl, Tesco, Asda) or Bockwurst sausages (Asda, Sainsbury) make a slightly healthier alternative and fit perfectly for my cheat at sausage rolls. These sausages have way less flavour than the British or Irish cousins, so I give them a little sage and onion flavouring before I wrap them in pastry.

INGREDIENTS

- 3-4 Bratwurst, Bockwurst or similar sausages
- 1 sheet of Puff pastry, (rectangular and not round)
- Ground sage
- Onion powder
- 1 medium-sized Egg

Serves	3-4
Difficulty	●○○
Functions	**Bake/Roast**
Time Prep	5
Time Cook	25

METHOD

1. Open and unwrap the puff pastry on a chopping board, in a landscape orientation. Situate 3 or 4 sausages at equal spaces so that each could be wrapped in the pastry.

2. Slice the pastry down the middle in both directions. So, to create 3 or 4 pieces of pastry that can wrap the sausage. Sprinkle some ground sage along the length of each sausage as well as some onion powder.

3. Wrap each sausage very loosely with the puff pastry and pinch the ends together so that the sausages stay in their pastry when lifted up. Score diagonal lines along each sausage roll to aid expansion when cooking.

4. Crack and beat an egg in a small cup. Select BAKE/ROAST on the Foodi to pre-heat the machine for 3 minutes at 170°C.

5. Position the steaming rack next to your workspace with the horizontal shelf nearest the bottom and top it with some grease proof paper (if you have some), or slightly grease the horizontal bars of the steaming rack.

6. Using a pastry brush, brush all sausage rolls with egg, turn them over, and brush them again until all parts are coated.

7. Transfer the sausage rolls onto the rack so that they do not touch one another.

8. Transfer the entire rack into the cooking pot.

9. Don't worry about egg dripping from the sausage rolls into the base of the cooking pot, it crisps very quickly during cooking so is easy to clean.

10. Again, select BAKE/ROAST and cook for 15 minutes at 170°C.

11. When the time is up, open the lid, carefully turn the sausage rolls over and cook again on the BAKE/ROAST function for a further 10 minutes, checking close to the end of the 10 minutes that nothing is burning.

12. I serve them with salad and some brown sauce. Enjoy.

TIP

You can also use vegetarian sausages with this recipe.

BACON-CHICKEN STICKS WITH WEDGES, CARROTS & BBQ DIP

INGREDIENTS

- 500g of Potatoes
- 4 Carrots
- 6 slices of Streaky bacon
- 2 Chicken breast fillets
- 2 tablespoons of Barbecue sauce

Serves	2-3
Difficulty	●●○
Functions	**Bake/roast Air crisp**
Time Prep	5
Time Cook	35

- 3 tablespoons of Cream
- 3 tablespoons of Natural yoghurt
- 1 teaspoon of ground Paprika
- Salt and Pepper to season
- Olive oil

METHOD

1. Boil a kettle of water.

2. Wash the potatoes and cut into 1cm wide potato wedges. Add to a large bowl. Drizzle about a dessert spoonful of olive oil into the bowl and a teaspoon of ground paprika. Toss the wedges well so that all wedges are coated in oil and paprika.

3. Put the air crisp basket into the Foodi cooking pot and tip the wedges into it. Select BAKE/ROAST and cook for 5 minutes at 180°C.

4. Peel the carrots and slice into ½ cm wide batons. In a saucepan, add the carrot batons and cover in boiling water from the kettle. Add a little salt and turn on a medium heat.

5. Slice each chicken breast lengthways into three. Dress each of the 6 strips of chicken in streaky bacon in a coil-like wrap. Make sure each piece of chicken is no thicker than 2cm (if thicker than 2cm, then you will need to increase the air crisp time later in the recipe to ensure the chicken is cooked)

6. In a small bowl, add the cream, yoghurt, a pinch of salt, a twist of black pepper and the barbecue sauce. Mix well with a fork to make the dip sauce. Divide into 2 or 3 small ramekins, depending on how many plates are going to be served.

7. Open the Foodi crisping lid, give the basket a little shake and add the bacon-wrapped chicken sticks on top of the potato wedges. The juices created by the cooking bacon will help flavour the wedges and mix well with the paprika coating. Select AIR CRISP and cook for 20 minutes at 190°C. In the last 5 minutes of the cooking time, open the lid to check that nothing is burning.

8. With the aid of a sieve or a colander, drain the water from the carrots and add a spoonful or two to each plate. Open the Foodi lid and remove the air basket, placing it onto a large plate to catch any dripping oil. Add 3 wrapped chicken sticks on 2 plates or 2 chicken sticks on 3 plates, depending on how many people are eating.

9. Shake the air crisp basket to loosen and coat the wedges and divide them onto the plates next to the chicken and the carrot batons. Add a ramekin of barbecue dip onto each plate and enjoy.

PERFECT LEG OF LAMB

INGREDIENTS

- 1.0 - 1.3kg leg of fresh Lamb

Serves	2-5
Difficulty	●○○
Functions	**Pressure** **Air crisp**
Time Prep	2
Time Cook	35

METHOD

1. Remove accessories from the cooking pot in place the leg of lamb inside. Add 250ml of water inside.

2. Fit the pressure lid and switch the vent dial to SEAL.

3. Select PRESSURE and pressure cook for 35 minutes on the high setting. When done, switch the vent dial to VENT to quick release the pressure.

4. Remove the pressure lid and close the built-in lid. Select AIR CRISP and cook at 200°C for 6 minutes.

5. Remove from the Foodi and wrap in aluminium foil for 10 minutes to rest. Carve and enjoy.

6. Keep any juices for a perfect gravy.

SINGAPORE CHICKEN

INGREDIENTS

- A 1.4 to 1.6kg whole Chicken
- 1 ½ tablespoons of Salt
- Pepper to season
- Butter
- 2 tablespoons of Soy sauce
- 1 Apple
- 2 tablespoons of Cornflour
- 2 tablespoons of Oyster sauce
- 2 tablespoons of Honey
- String or cotton to tie the chicken legs and wings together

Serves	3-5
Difficulty	●●○
Functions	Pressure Sear/Sauté Air crisp
Time Prep	6 ¼ hours
Time Cook	35

METHOD

1. Remove a bag of innards from the chicken. Take a large bowl and add 500ml of cold water. Add a tablespoon of salt to the water, stir it around and sink the chicken in it. Place the bowl in the refrigerator for at least 2 hours. Remove the bowl from the refrigerator and pour away the water.

2. In a small bowl mix 2 tablespoons of soy sauce, 2 tablespoons of oyster sauce, 2 tablespoons of honey, a twist of black pepper and 1 teaspoon of salt together. Massage the chicken with this marinade. When all outside parts of the chicken are covered in the marinade, put the bowl with the chicken back into the refrigerator. Leave to marinate for 4 hours.

3. Remove the bowl from the fridge. Cut an apple into eighths and stuff the apple segments into the cavity of the chicken. Tie the legs of the chicken together with a piece of string or cotton. Do the same for the wings.

4. Open the Foodi bult-in lid and remove the air crisp basket. Add 150ml of water and the remainder of the marinade from the bowl to the cooking pot. Try to get as much of the marinade out of the bowl as possible using a silicone spatula.

5. Place the steaming rack into the cooking pot with the horizontal part nearest the bottom. Place the chicken onto the steaming rack breast side upwards and install the pressure lid.

6. Switch the vent dial to SEAL and select PRESSURE. Pressure cook using the high setting for 18 minutes. When the countdown timer has reached zero, switch the vent dial to VENT and allow the pressure to release quickly. Remove the pressure lid.

7. Melt a tablespoon of butter in a saucepan and mix it with the honey to form a rudimental glaze. With the aid of a brush, coat the top of the chicken with the glaze. Close the built-in lid and select AIR CRISP. Cook for 6 minutes at 200°C.

8. Remove the chicken from the pot and place it carefully onto a large plate, leaving the liquid in the pot. Select SEAR/SAUTÉ using the high setting and heat up the liquid. Add 2 tablespoons of cornflour and 2 tablespoons of water into a cup, mix well together. Add to the sauce and stir well until the sauce thickens.

9. Pour the resulting sauce over the top of the chicken and get ready to blow your mind.

VEGAN YELLOW CURRY WITH BEANS & JASMINE RICE ⓥ

* INGREDIENTS

- 2 Carrots
- 200g of Green beans
- 150g of Jasmine rice
- 1 Lime
- 3 dessert spoons of Yellow curry paste

Serves	2-3
Difficulty	●●○
Functions	Sear/Sauté
Time Prep	5
Time Cook	30

- 2 Spring onions
- 200g of fresh Button mushrooms
- 1 teaspoon of Vegetable stock powder / vegetable stock cube or vegetable OXO cube
- 250ml of Coconut milk
- 1 Garlic clove
- Salt & Pepper
- Olive oil

METHOD

1. Boil a kettle with plenty of water in it.

2. Wash and chop the mushrooms into quarters.

3. Peel the carrots and chop into 1cm thick slices.

4. Wash then top and tail the green beans, cut them all in half after that.

5. Cut the roots end of the spring onions away and cut the rest into thin rings. Keep the green and white parts separate. The green parts will be used for decoration.

6. Peel the garlic and chop finely, do not crush.

7. Take a measuring jug with 50ml of boiling water and add the vegetable stock, stirring until fully dissolved.

8. Prepare rice in a saucepan with a lid. (1 cup of rice to every 1 1/2 cups of boiling water, rinse the rice in a sieve, boil in the water. As soon as the rice has reached the boil, allow it to boil for 1 minute.

9. Reduce the heat to the lowest setting and cover with a lid. Cook slowly without removing the lid for exactly 10 minutes. Turn off the heat and leave sealed closed for a further 12 minutes. Do not open the lid at any point and make sure the saucepan lid seals completely – ie, not a lid with a hole in it). As the rice is cooking, carry on with the recipe for the curry.

10. Remove accessories from the cooking pot of the Foodi. Select SEAR/SAUTÉ on the medium temperature setting and add a dessert spoon of olive oil to the pot.

11. When the oil is hot, add the white parts of the spring onions and the chopped garlic. Stir well and cook for 2 minutes.

12. Add the yellow curry paste and continue to stir for a further minute.

13. Add the prepared vegetable stock and the coconut milk.

Let it heat up before adding the carrots, green beans and the mushrooms.

14. Reduce the temperature to low and cook for 12 minutes until the vegetables are softened somewhat. Carry on with the recipe in the meantime. Cut the lime in half. Cut the chili in half and remove the seeds. Chop into fine strips.

15. Press one half of the lime into the curry and slice the other half into quarters. Season with salt and pepper.

16. After the rice has cooked, open the lid and loosen the rice with a fork. Serve the rice onto 2 or 3 deep plates or bowls.

17. Dish curry out next to the rice and cover the dish with the green parts of the spring onion as decoration. For those who want them, add the red chili strips to the top of the curry. Enjoy.

* DOUBLE THE INGREDIENTS TO SERVE MORE:

Due to the height of the side-walls of the cooking pot, and the fact that the sear/sauté function cooks from all sides, you can double the ingredients amount of all ingredients without needing to alter the cooking times at all.

DID YOU KNOW?

You can double amount of water and rice but NOT double the cooking time. So instead of cooking 1 cup of jasmine rice and a cup of water, cool 2 cups of jasmine rice with 2 cups of water.
Keep the timing exactly the same.

BLACK & SPICY CHICKEN BREAST FILLETS

INGREDIENTS

- 2 chicken breasts (roughly 340g)
- 2 teaspoons of paprika
- 1 teaspoon of ground cumin
- 1 teaspoon of dried thyme
- 1 teaspoon of cayenne pepper
- 1 teaspoon of black pepper
- 1 teaspoon of onion powder
- Salt
- 1 dessert spoon of olive oil

Serves	4-6
Difficulty	●●○
Functions	**Air crisp**
Time Prep	2
Time Cook	35

METHOD

1. Add to a small bowl the thyme, cumin, paprika, cayenne, black pepper and salt. Mix together well with a fork. Take the chicken breasts and remove any parts of the chicken that you would not normally eat.

2. Add the chicken breasts into a deep bowl and add the small glug of oil. Toss so that each breast is coated fully. Throw in the spice mixture and turn the chicken thoroughly so that each breast is fully covered. Let it marinate for 5 or more minutes. Add the air crisp basket to the Foodi cooking pot and place the chicken into it.

3. Select AIR CRISP and cook at 180°C for 10 minutes Open the lid and turn the chicken over. Close the lid and air crisp for a further 10 minutes.

4. Transfer to a large plate, tipping any juices onto the place first, cover with aluminium foil and let them rest for 5 minutes before serving.

LAMB CHOPS WITH ROSEMARY

INGREDIENTS

- 1-2 Lamb chops, sprayed with oil.
- A handful of fresh rosemary

Serves	1-2
Difficulty	●○○
Functions	**Air crisp**
Time Prep	1
Time Cook	23

METHOD

1. Pre-heat the Foodi using the BAKE/ROAST function for 3 minutes. Add 1 or 2 lamb chops to the air crisp basket and place some chopped rosemary on the top of the chops. Place the air crisp basket into the Foodi.

2. Select AIR CRISP and cook for 20 minutes at 170°C and let it rest for 10 minutes wrapped in foil after the cooking time.

CHOPPED CHICKEN IN CREAMY CURRY SAUCE

* INGREDIENTS

- 3 Carrots
- 600g of Potatoes
- 1 Garlic clove
- 1 Spring onion
- 150g of Green beans
- 200g (200ml) of Double cream

Serves	2-3
Difficulty	●●○
Functions	Sear/Sauté Pressure
Time Prep	10
Time Cook	45

- 1 teaspoon of Honey
- 2 Chicken breast fillets
- 1 teaspoon of Curry powder
- 1 teaspoon of Chicken stock powder / 1 chicken stock cube or 1 OXO stock cube
- Salt & Pepper
- Olive oil

METHOD

1. Boil a kettle of water. Wash the potatoes and cut them into mouth-sized chunks. Tip the potatoes into the air crisp basket and place the basket into the cooking pot. Add 250ml of water to the base of the cooking pot and fit the pressure lid. SEAL the vent and select PRESSURE. Cook on the high setting for 4 minutes.

2. Continue with the recipe as the potatoes are cooking. Peel the carrots and slice them into thin slices. Peel the garlic and chop finely. Chop the spring onion into thin rings. Keep the green parts separate from the white rings. Top and tail the ends of the green beans and chop them into 3.

3. Take a measuring jug and add 100ml of boiling water together with the chicken stock. Stir to dissolve. Add the cream, honey and curry powder. Mix well.

4. Chop the chicken breast fillets into thin strips. After the countdown timer reaches zero, switch the vent dial to VENT and allow the pressure to release. Remove the lid when all pressure has released. Remove the air crisp basket and keep it to the side until later.

5. Empty any water from the cooking pot. Select SEAR/SAUTÉ using the high setting. Add a dessert spoon of olive oil and when the oil is hot, add the chicken. Remove from the pot when browned. Again, add a dessert spoon of olive oil to the pot and add the carrots, the chopped garlic, the white spring onion and the green beans. Stir for 3-4 minutes. Add the sauce from the measuring jug and stir well. Cook for a further 6 minutes. The sauce should thicken.

6. Add the chicken and the potatoes back to the pot and carefully mix with the sauce. Cook for a further 3 minutes. Season with salt & pepper, serve into 2 or 3 deep plates and decorate each with the green spring onion. Enjoy.

* DOUBLE THE INGREDIENTS TO SERVE MORE:

Due to the height of the side-walls of the cooking pot, and the fact that the sear/sauté function cooks from all sides, you can double the ingredients amount of all ingredients without needing to alter the cooking times at all.

KING PRAWNS

INGREDIENTS

- 16 King Prawns (frozen)
- Olive oil
- Salt

Serves	3-4
Difficulty	●○○
Functions	**Air crisp** **Pressure**
Time Prep	**1**
Time Cook	**10**

METHOD

1. If not already peeled and de-veined, peel the king prawns and remove the veins.

2. Place the prawns on the steaming rack with the surface of the rack closest to the top of the Foodi

3. Add 250ml of water to the base of the cooking pot.

4. Fit the pressure lid and switch the vent dial to SEAL

5. Select PRESSURE. Pressure cook on the high setting for 0 minutes. Yes, zero minutes. The pressure-cooking is finished as soon as high-pressure is reached.

6. Quick release pressure by switching the vent dial to VENT. When pressure has been fully released, remove the pressure lid.

7. Brush the prawns lightly with olive oil and season lightly with salt.

8. Close the built-in lid and select AIR CRISP. Cook for 5 minutes at 200°C.

CHICKEN & LEEK PIE

INGREDIENTS

- 10 sheets of Filo pastry (or 1 roll of puff-pastry)
- 3-4 Chicken breast fillets
- 1 Leek
- 2 large Carrots
- 1 stick of Celery (optional)
- 2 Garlic cloves
- 1 handful of fresh Thyme (or 1 tablespoon of dried thyme)
- 1 handful of fresh parsley (or 1 tablespoon of dried parsley)
- 1 bag of Baby spinach leaves
- 1 Chicken stock cube or 1 chicken OXO cube
- 250ml of Whole milk
- 2 tablespoons of Butter
- 2 tablespoons of Plain flour
- 2 tablespoons of Wholegrain mustard
- Salt & Pepper

Serves	4-5
Difficulty	●●○
Functions	Sear/Sauté Bake/Roast
Time Prep	10
Time Cook	35

METHOD

1. Remove the pastry from the refrigerator and allow to get to room temperature while covered in a damp tea-towel.
2. If you are using puff-pastry, roll out the pastry and put the cooking pot base down onto it. Use a knife to cut a circle out slightly larger than the base of the pot. Careful with scratching work surfaces with the knife!
3. Chop the chicken breasts up into mouth-sized chunks. Remove the base of the leek and slice down the full length. Stack all parts of the leek together and wash under a tap. Slice the leek into 2cm long slices.
4. Peel and dice the carrots.
5. Finely shop the celery into thin half-moons.
6. Peel and crush the garlic into a small bowl.
7. Wash and pluck the fresh herbs from their stalks. Finely chop the parsley. Keep them separated.
8. In the cooking pot of the Foodi, add a dessert spoon of olive oil and use the SEAR/SAUTÉ to heat it up using the medium temperature setting.
9. When the oil is hot, add the chicken (in two batches if you don't wish to keep stirring) and cook until slightly browned. Transfer the chicken to a deep bowl for use later.
10. Again, add a quick splash of oil. Add the leek, carrot and celery and cook, stirring, for 5 minutes, or until softened.
11. Add the garlic, thyme, parsley and baby spinach leaves and cook, stirring, for 2-3 minutes, or until fragrant and softened.
12. Transfer the vegetables to the deep bowl containing the chicken.
13. In a measuring jug, add 50ml of water and crumble the stock cube / add the stock powder to it. Stir well. Add the milk.
14. In the cooking pot, melt the butter and slowly stir-in the plain flour. Cook on the medium setting for 1 minute, constantly stirring.
15. Slowly add the stock and milk mix stirring all the time until there are no lumps. Cook for 5 minutes until the sauce has thickened. Stir in the mustard and season with salt and pepper.

16. Add the chicken and the vegetables to the sauce and fold everything well with a large wooden spoon so that everything is covered in sauce.

17. Scrunch each filo pastry sheet into very loose balls and place on top of the pie. Repeat until the whole pie is covered, making sure not to overcrowd the pastry. Or, if you are using puff-pastry, spray lightly the walls of the cooking pot with oil and with the aid of a rolling-pin, drape the pastry over the rolling-pin and slowly place over the top of the sauce, pressing the edges down with your index finger.

18. Regardless which pastry you are using, spray it slightly with an oil spray if you have one or use a basting brush to lightly brush the top of the pastry with either olive oil, milk or egg, your choice.

19. Close the built-in lid and select BAKE/ROAST. Cook for 10 minutes at 180°C. After the time has surpassed, if the pastry is not golden brown, select AIR CRISP and cook at 200°C for a further few minutes.

20. Carefully use a plastic or silicone spatula to unseal the edges of the pastry from the walls of the cooking pot, then use a large spoon or fish slice to serve the pie. If using a knife to cut the pastry, be sure not to dig in too deep as the coating of the cooking pot must not be touched with a metal knife.

FILLET STEAK

INGREDIENTS

- 2 Steak fillets
- Olive oil
- Seasoning, such as cracked black pepper and salt

Serves	2
Difficulty	●○○
Functions	**Air crisp**
Time Prep	**1**
Time Cook	**15**

METHOD

1. Pre-heat the Foodi with the air crisp basket inside the cooking pot by selecting BAKE/ROAST for 3 minutes.

2. With some olive oil on your hands, rub the steaks so that every part is slightly oiled. Season with your preferred seasoning, such as lots of cracked black pepper and sea salt.

3. Place the steak fillets into the air crisp basket, ideally so that they do not overlap and close the lid. Select AIR CRISP and cook at 200°C for approximately 12 minutes, depending on how you want them cooked. 12 minutes works best for medium, 10 minutes for rare, 13 minutes for medium-well and 14 minutes for well done.

TIP

Use a meat thermometer to establish how well the steaks are cooked. Rare (52°C), Medium-rare (57°C), Medium (63°C), Medium-well (66°C) and Well (69°C)

INDIAN SHEPHERD'S PIE

INGREDIENTS

- 4-5 large Baking potatoes
- 400g of Minced lamb
- 2 Garlic cloves
- 1 Red chili
- 2 tablespoons of Garam Masala
- 1 ½ cans of Chopped tomatoes
- 1 tablespoon of ground Turmeric
- 2 Onions
- 3 large Carrots
- Side-salad to serve with
- Salt & Pepper
- Knob of butter
- Splash of milk
- Olive oil

Serves	4-5
Difficulty	●●○
Functions	Pressure Grill Sear/sauté
Time Prep	5
Time Cook	50

METHOD

1. Remove accessories from the cooking pot. Wash the potatoes (do not peel them) and slice them into 2cm - 3cm cubes. Place the potatoes into the cooking pot. Add 250ml of water. Fit the pressure cooker lid, turn the vent dial to SEAL. Select PRESSURE and cook on HIGH for 20 minutes.

2. Peel, halve and dice the onions. Wash and then trim the ends off the carrots. Cut them into ½ cm wide batons, halving them after they have been sliced. Peel the garlic cloves. Cut the chili in half lengthways and remove the seeds. Chop the chili halves widthways into 2mm wide strips.

3. Prepare lettuce leaves and any other salad items that you will serve with the pie. Crush the garlic in a bowl.

4. After the potato has finished cooking, switch the vent dial to the VENT position to release the pressure. Remove the potatoes from the Foodi, draining any residual water using a colander or a sieve. Pour the potatoes into a bowl or saucepan, add a knob of butter and a splash of milk, the turmeric too and season with a little salt. Use a potato masher to mash the potato to a light fluffy puree.

5. In the empty cooking pot, splash a little oil and select SEAR/SAUTE using the high temperature setting. When the oil is hot, throw in the lamb mince and break it up with a wooden spoon. When the mince has browned, tip the mince into a bowl. Spoon-off any fat.

6. Use the SEAR/SAUTE medium heat setting without any more fat added (as there should be some fat in the cooking pot) and throw in the onion and carrots. Cook for about 6 minutes under regular stirring. Add the garam masala, the crushed garlic and the chili, still stirring for another 2 minutes.

7. Add the canned tomatoes and the lamb mince, mixing everything in well. If it is starting to look a little dry, add a few splashes of water. Season with salt and pepper. When the sauce has thickened, add a layer of mashed potato on the top and ruffle it with a fork to make ridges to aid crisping.

8. Select GRILL and cook for 5 minutes, so that the top has browned and crisped. Plate up with salad. Enjoy.

SPICY CHICKEN CASSEROLE

INGREDIENTS

- 2 Red peppers
- 300g/300ml of Crème fraiche
- 1 Garlic clove
- 1 tablespoon of Sriracha sauce
- 2 teaspoons of Chicken stock powder / 2 chicken stock cube or chicken OXO cubes
- 400g Chickpeas (2 cartons)
- 4 Chicken breast fillets
- 1 can of Pomodorini cherry tomatoes
- 10g or 2 dessert spoons of roasted Pumpkin seeds
- 1 bunch of fresh Parsley
- Salt & pepper to season
- Olive oil

Serves	4-5
Difficulty	●●○
Functions	**Sear/sauté**
Time Prep	**10**
Time Cook	**40**

METHOD

1. Boil a kettle with plenty of water in it. Slice the peppers in half and remove the seeds. Chop into 3cm long strips. Use a sieve to wash the chickpeas until the water under the sieve runs clear. Pluck the leaves from the parsley and chop finely. Take the chicken breast fillets and chop into mouth-sized chunks. Peel the garlic clove and chop very finely, but do not crush.

2. In a measuring jug, add 600ml of boiling water and the chicken stock. Stir until dissolved. Keep for later.

3. Remove the accessories from the Foodi cooking pot. Select SEAR/SAUTÉ on the high setting. Add 2 dessert spoons of olive oil, the garlic and the pepper slices. Sauté for 8 minutes, stirring often. Change the temperature setting to the low temperature setting.

4. Add the pomodorini tomatoes and the chicken stock from above. Cook for 15 minutes and use a frying pan lid to cover the pot. If you do not have such a lid, use a large plate, assuming that it is heatproof.

5. When the vegetables are soft, add the sriracha sauce, season with salt and pepper and if you have some to hand, add a pinch of sugar. Transfer the contents to a large jug or bowl. Stir in the crème fraiche. Use a hand mixer to purify the mixture, keeping it in the jug or bowl afterwards.

6. Quickly swill the Foodi cooking pot, place it back in and select SEAR/SAUTÉ on the high setting. Add a tablespoon of olive oil. When the oil is hot, add the chicken and the chickpeas. Cook for about 3 minutes, stirring well, until the chicken is not pink any more.

7. Add the jug or bowl of purified vegetables to the pot and let everything warm up fully. Serve into 4 or 5 deep plates or bowls, top with parsley and pumpkin seeds. Enjoy this low-in-carbohydrates feast.

AIR CRISPED ROASTED CHICKEN

INGREDIENTS

- 1 medium sized fresh chicken (roughly 1.4kg)
- Olive oil
- 1 Lemon or lemon juice
- 1 tablespoon of Honey

Serves	4
Difficulty	●○○
Functions	**Air crisp**
Time Prep	1
Time Cook	**60**

1. In a small bowl, mix a tablespoon of honey with the juice of a lemon. Mix it well and add a glug of olive oil. Use a pastry brush to glaze the breast side of the chicken with the honey.

2. Place the oiled chicken (with all innards removed) onto the steaming rack, where the steaming rack grill surface is closest to the base of the cooking pot, OR ideally if the chicken will fit, use the air crisp basket. The air crisp basket allows for even movement of heat as well as cooking from the base via the propeller shape of the detachable diffuser.

3. Season with chicken seasoning if required. There is no need to turn the chicken during cooking as the Foodi

cooks evenly all around.

Select AIR CRISP and cook for 60 minutes at 185°C. Use a meat thermometer to check that at the thickest part of the chicken, the internal temperature is equal to or greater than 75°C to be sure that it is indeed cooked. Remove the chicken from the Foodi and wrap in aluminium foil. Leave to rest on a plate for at least 15 minutes.

CHEESE & HAM TOASTIES

INGREDIENTS

- Mayonnaise
- Unsmoked Ham
- Dijon mustard
- 4 or 6 slices of wholemeal or seeded sliced bread
- Gruyere, aged Gouda or vintage Cheddar Cheese

Serves	1-2
Difficulty	○○○
Functions	**Air crisp**
Time Prep	5
Time Cook	7

METHOD

1. Simply spread Dijon mustard on one side of each slice of bread. Layer half of the bread slices with cheese almost but-not-quite to the edge of the bread. Layer further with slices of ham. Cover with the slices that are not loaded with cheese or ham. Spread the outside of the sandwiches lightly with mayonnaise and slice diagonally in half.

2. Put on the steaming rack, where the base of the rack is at the lowest position. Place the rack in the cooking pot. Select AIR CRISP and cook at 200°C for 7 minutes.

BONED & SKINNED CHICKEN THIGHS

INGREDIENTS

- 4 chicken thighs (fresh 180 to 250g in weight)
- Olive oil
- Cracked black pepper
- Sea salt

Serves	4
Difficulty	●○○
Functions	**Pressure Air crisp**
Time Prep	1
Time Cook	15

METHOD

1. Place the chicken thighs in the air crisp basked of the Foodi and place the basket into the cooking pot.

2. Add 250ml of water to the base of the cooking pot. Fit the pressure lid and switch the vent dial to SEAL

3. Select PRESSURE. Pressure cook on the high setting for 2 minutes. Yes, just 2 minutes. The pressure-cooking is finished at 2 minutes after high-pressure is reached.

4. Quick release pressure by switching the vent dial to VENT. When pressure has been fully released, remove the pressure lid.

5. Brush the chicken thighs lightly with olive oil. Season with sea salt and cracked black pepper. Close the built-in lid and select AIR CRISP. Cook for 10 minutes at 200°C, checking for burning after 8 minutes.

QUICKER ROASTED CHICKEN

This recipe is for a roughly 1.4kg fresh whole chicken. The difference between this recipe and the previous recipe is that with this recipe, the time to complete is greatly reduced and that the meat is literally fall-off-the-bone succulent and much juicier.

Serves	3-5
Difficulty	●○○
Functions	**Pressure**
	Air crisp
Time Prep	1
Time Cook	35

The chicken skin is not as crispy as with the standard roast chicken recipe but if you season the skin well and oil it before the air crisp stage, it can be very crispy indeed. Personally, my family and I much prefer this recipe, especially when cooked for part of a Sunday roast dinner. The juices make for amazing gravy too.

INGREDIENTS

- 1 medium sized fresh chicken (roughly 1.4kg)
- Olive oil
- Seasoning (optional)

METHOD

1. For a 1.4kg chicken, take the chicken at least half an hour before cooking from the refrigerator then place the chicken without its innards inside the air crisp basket, breast facing upwards.

2. Put one full cup of water into the cooking pot. Add a chicken stock cube and let it dissolve in the water in the base of the cooking pot.

3. Add the air crisp basket (complete with chicken) into the Foodi cooking pot. Fit the pressure cooker lid and select PRESSURE. Make sure the vent setting is set to SEAL.

4. Pressure cook for 15 minutes on the high setting. It will take a few minutes to reach the required cooking pressure before the countdown timer starts.

5. After the countdown has reached zero, let the pressure slowly and naturally release until the timer counts up to five minutes.

6. After the five minutes of natural release, switch the vent to VENT on the lid and be careful as hot steam releases from the vent.

7. After successful release of all pressure, the lid may be opened. Remove the lid and carefully rub olive oil into the skin of the top of the chicken. Optionally add chicken seasoning to the breast and thighs of the chicken. Leave the water in the base of the cooking pot, this can be later used for making a gravy or a sauce of your choice.

8. Close the built-in lid and select AIR CRISP. Cook for 15 minutes on the default 200°C temperature. Occasionally in the last five minutes of cooking, open the lid to check if the chicken is cooking as it should be, namely that it is not burning. For extra crispy skin, this cooking time may be increased without affecting the succulency of the meat too much.

9. Carefully, with the aid of a large plate, remove the basket

and chicken after the cooking has completed. Rest the chicken in aluminum foil for at least ten minutes. Additional hot juices may be inside the carcass of the chicken, another aid for gravy-making.

TIPS

Be careful removing the chicken as it is literally fall-off-the-bone, you may end up with just a handful of bones when lifting it! I tend to use a large wooden spoon inside the ribcage of the chicken to aid lifting it out of the air crisp basket.

Smaller chickens and larger chickens will of course require a different amount of time when it comes to pressure cooking. 1.1kg takes 12 minutes to pressure cook but an extra 2 minutes of natural release (as quick release affects the stringiness of the meat).

A 1.6kg chicken takes 20 minutes of pressure cooking.

Add butter underneath the skin of the fresh chicken as a compound if you wish to have a much juicier resulting meat.

The resulting water/oil/juice mix at the base of the cooking pot may be strained with a sieve and poured into a saucepan. Excess fat may be removed with the aid of a spoon. Add a sprig of each rosemary and thyme, then bring the drippings to a simmer, thicken as needed with corn flour.

Before I start cooking the chicken in the pressure cooker stage, I pressure cook for five minutes potatoes. Each potato cut into quarters and with 250ml of water at the base before starting the pressure cooker. After its finished, I pressure cook the chicken. When that's complete, I air crisp the potatoes having mixed them with a little sunflower oil as the chicken was cooking. After the air crisp has done a fairly good job at crisping the potatoes up, I tip them into a large Pyrex dish, put them into a warm oven and continue to cook

the chicken with the second phase of the recipe, the air crisp phase.

The pressure cooker water from the chicken together with the starchy water from the potatoes makes for a great gravy base and the starch will later help to thicken the gravy as it reaches boiling point.

BUFFALO WINGS

INGREDIENTS

- 6-10 frozen Buffalo chicken wings
- Optional barbecue sauce

Serves	1-2
Difficulty	●○○
Functions	**Air crisp**
Time Prep	**0**
Time Cook	**23**

METHOD

1. Pre-heat the Foodi by selecting the BAKE/ROAST program for 3 minutes.

2. Place the frozen chicken wings into the air crisp basket. Insert the basket into the cooking pot.

3. Select AIR CRISP and cook at 180°C for 20 minutes. Open occasionally to shake the wings around in the basket.

SWEET & SOUR CHICKEN

Ingredients

 2 Chicken breast filets

 2 Spring onions

 1 Onion

 Olive oil

 150g Jasmine rice (or basmati rice)

Serves	2-3
Difficulty	●○○
Functions	Sear/Sauté
Time Prep	5
Time Cook	40

 2 Red / Orange or Yellow peppers

 10g or 3 teaspoons full of Sesame seeds

 1 tablespoon of Cornflour

 3 dessert spoons of Mango chutney

 1 Vegetable stock cubes or OXO vegetable stock cube

 2 tablespoons / sachets of Tomato ketchup

 1 ½ tablespoons of Soy sauce

 1 tablespoon of Red wine vinegar

- Salt & Pepper
- Kettle of boiling water

1. Prepare rice in a saucepan with a lid. (1 cup of rice (200g) to every 1 ½ cups of water (350ml), rinse the rice in a sieve, boil in the water. As soon as the rice has reached the boil, allow it to boil for 1 minute. Reduce the heat to the lowest setting and cover with a lid. Cook slowly without removing the lid for exactly 10 minutes. Turn off the heat and leave sealed closed for a further 12 minutes. Do not open the lid at any point and make sure the saucepan lid seals completely – ie, not a lid with a hole in it). As the rice is cooking, carry on with the recipe for the curry.

2. Remove accessories from the Foodi. Turn on the Foodi by selecting SEAR/SAUTÉ using the high setting.

3. Cut the pepper in half and remove the seeds. Slice length ways into strips and cut each strip into a few pieces.

4. Chop the chicken breasts into 1cm wide strips. In a bowl, add 1 tablespoon of cornflour, a pinch or two of salt and pepper and mix with a spoon. Add the chicken breast strips and stir well until all parts of the chicken are coated

5. Without adding any fat or oil, add the sesame seeds to the base of the food and spread them out. Allow to cook for a minute or two. Empty the cooking pot into a small bowl for use later. Return the cooking pot to the Foodi.

6. In a measuring jug, add 200ml of boiling water and a vegetable/OXO stock cube. Stir to aid dissolving. Keep for later.

7. Wash the spring onion, cut off any roots and slice into small rings, storing white parts on one side of the chopping board, green on another side (the green parts are for decoration).

8. Peel the onion, halve it and slice it into small wedges.

9. In another bowl, add 2 tablespoons of tomato ketchup, 3 dessert spoons of mango chutney, 1 tablespoon of red wine vinegar (do not use malt vinegar), 1 ½ tablespoons of soy sauce, half a dessert spoon of sugar and mix well.

10. Add a tablespoon of olive oil to the cooking pot and allow to warm through on the SEAR/SAUTÉ high setting.

11. When the oil is hot, add the white parts of the spring onion rings, the onion wedges and the flour-coated chicken. Stirring, cook for 3 to 5 minutes.

12. Add the pepper slices and cook together for a further minute.

13. Add the ketchup-soy-sauce mix, together with the vegetable stock. Stir well and cook for 5 minutes, until the sauce has thickened a little. Season with salt and pepper if needed.

14. When everything is done, serve a large portion of rice on the side of each plate and half of the sweet and sour next to it.

15. Decorate with the sesame seeds with the remaining green parts of the spring onion. Enjoy.

GNOCCHI WITH BACON & TOMATO-SPINACH SAUCE

* INGREDIENTS

- 2 Spring onions
- 280g of Cherry tomatoes
- 8 rashers of back Bacon or 12 rashers of streaky bacon (swap bacon for 100g of mushrooms if you wish to make a vegetarian version)

Serves	4
Difficulty	●○○
Functions	**Sear/Sauté**
Time Prep	5
Time Cook	25

- 300ml of Crème fraiche
- 100g of Baby spinach (1 bag)
- 800g of fresh Gnocchi (or baby dumplings, or Swabian pasta, they all work with this recipe)
- 80g of Sliced parmesan / Italian hard cheese
- 8g of Chicken stock or a chicken stock cube / chicken OXO cube
- Pepper
- Olive oil

METHOD

1. Chop the cherry tomatoes in half.

2. Wash the spring onions and cut off the roots. Slice into fine rings.

3. Cut the bacon, fat and all, into 1cm wide strips.

4. Wash the baby spinach.

5. Open the Foodi lid and remove accessories. Add a tablespoon of olive oil to the cooking pot and select SEAR/SAUTE using the high setting.

6. When the oil is hot, toss in the Gnocchi or equivalent. Stir them around occasionally. When they are brown and crispy on the outside, remove the pot from the Foodi with the aid of a thick cloth, empty the pot into a deep bowl/plate and keep for later.

7. Return the cooking pot into the Foodi, select SEAR/SAUTE again and set the temperature to the high setting. Do not add any oil.

8. Throw in the bacon strips and stir occasionally so that the bacon crisps up well, around 6 minutes. The fat around the bacon will also either diminish or crisp up, depending on how much there is.

9. Reduce the temperature to the medium setting and add the spring onions and the tomatoes.

10. Add a fair few pinches of pepper. Stir well. Let it cook for a further 2 to 3 minutes, until the tomatoes start to lose their form and the spring onions become aromatic.

11. Add about 4 or 5 tablespoons of water as well as the crème fraiche. Stir in the chicken stock, crumbling it first if it is a stock cube.

12. Add the gnocchi back into the pot and stir it in well so that all parts are covered in the sauce. Slowly introduce small handfuls of baby spinach, slowly turning it into the sauce mix and adding more. When all the spinach has been added, switch off the heat.

13. Prepare 4 deep plates or bowls and dish out the meal. Add sprinkles of the slices of hard cheese/parmesan to the top for extra flavour. Enjoy.

TIP

If you wish to make a vegetarian version of this recipe, simply swap the bacon for mushrooms at exactly the same stage and cook for the same time too. Just make sure that the mushrooms are cut quite finely.

* HALVE OR DOUBLE THE INGREDIENTS TO SERVE LESS OR MORE:

Due to the height of the side-walls of the cooking pot, and the fact that the sear/sauté function cooks from all sides, you can either halve or double the ingredients amount of all ingredients without needing to alter the cooking times at all.

DID YOU KNOW?

You can re-heat chips or fast-food fries that have gone cold or not eaten in the Ninja Foodi?

Don't throw them away!

Just select the AIR CRISP function and cook for a few minutes at 180°C

SALMON FILLETS

INGREDIENTS

- 2 Salmon fillets (frozen)
- Olive oil
- Salt
- Salad to serve

Serves	2
Difficulty	●○○
Functions	**Air crisp**
Time Prep	1
Time Cook	13

1. Brush the fillets lightly with olive oil and season well with salt.

2. Place them in the air crisp basket with the skin side (if there is skin) facing downwards.

3. Close the built-in lid and select AIR CRISP at 200°C. Cook for between 10 to 13 minutes. There is no need to turn the fillets during cooking.

PORK CHOPS

INGREDIENTS

- 4 Pork chops (boneless, frozen, between 180 to 250g)
- Olive oil
- Cracked black pepper
- Sea salt

Serves	4
Difficulty	●○○
Functions	**Pressure** **Air crisp**
Time Prep	1
Time Cook	20

METHOD

1. Place the chops on the steaming rack with the surface of the rack closest to the top of the Foodi. Add 250ml of water to the base of the cooking pot. Fit the pressure lid and switch the vent dial to SEAL

2. Select PRESSURE. Pressure cook on the high setting for 2 minutes. Yes, just 2 minutes. The pressure-cooking is finished at 2 minutes after high-pressure is reached.

3. Quick release pressure by switching the vent dial to VENT. When pressure has been fully released, remove the pressure lid.

4. Brush the chops lightly with olive oil. Season with sea salt and cracked black pepper. Close the built-in lid and select AIR CRISP. Cook for 10 to 15 minutes at 200°C, checking for burning after 10 minutes.

HERBY GARLIC-LEMON CHICKEN

INGREDIENTS

- 1 medium sized fresh chicken (roughly 1.4kg)
- 2 Lemons
- 1 tablespoon of Black peppercorns
- 3 tablespoons of Honey
- 4 or 5 garlic cloves
- 1 tablespoon of Olive oil
- Fresh thyme or rosemary (but not both)
- Salt
- Pepper

Serves	3-5
Difficulty	●●○
Functions	Pressure Air crisp
Time Prep	5
Time Cook	35

METHOD

1. Take the fresh chicken (without its innards) and swill briefly under low pressure cold water if required.

2. In a bowl, use a grater to zest both lemons. Cut the lemons in half and juice all four halves.

3. Add 150ml of boiling water from a kettle. Add the honey and a tablespoon of salt. Open the lid of the Foodi and throw in the bowl of seasonings, together with a few sprigs of thyme OR rosemary.

4. Peel all of the garlic cloves and using the flat edge of a kitchen knife to squash each clove flat without slicing them open. Add them to the pot.

5. Place the chicken breast-side upwards into the air crisp basket and put it into the cooking pot.

6. Install the pressure lid and switch the vent dial to SEAL

7. Select PRESSURE and pressure cook the contents on the high setting for 20 minutes.

8. After the countdown timer reaches zero, allow the timer to count-up to 5 minutes. This is a slow or natural release of pressure.

9. After 5 minutes, switch the vent dial to VENT and allow remaining pressure to escape from the Foodi. Remove the pressure lid.

10. Use a brush to apply olive oil to the skin at the top of the chicken OR use a vegetable oil spray to coat all parts of the top of the chicken.

11. Close the built-in lid and select AIR CRISP

12. Cook at 200°C for 10 minutes. Check regularly after 5 minutes that the chicken is not burning.

13. Remove the air crisp basket and carefully transfer the chicken to a large plate. Cover with aluminium foil and let it rest for 10 minutes. Any juices resting on the plate will be soaked up by the meat and will greatly influence flavour. Carve and enjoy.

DID YOU KNOW?

American versions of the machine have a BROIL button. This is called GRILL on the European version. So, if you're following an American recipe, just remember that broil = grill!

BANGERS 'N MASH WITH CABBAGE ON THE SIDE

INGREDIENTS

- 4 Pork / Irish sausages
- 3 Large Potatoes
- 1 Large carrot
- A bunch of fresh parsley
- 100g Cheddar cheese
- 2 dessert spoons of Wholegrain mustard
- 2 Red onions
- 8g Plain flour (1 dessert spoon)
- 2 dessert spoons of Tomato puree
- 1 Red wine stock pot
- 60g Pancetta lardons or 2 rashers of finely chopped bacon
- ½ a Savoy cabbage
- 250ml water
- A glug of Whole milk
- Salt
- Pepper

Serves	2-3
Difficulty	●●○
Functions	Sear/Sauté Air crisp
Time Prep	5
Time Cook	45

METHOD

1. Slice the cabbage into 1cm wide strips

2. Trim the carrot top and bottom, then thinly slice into thin circular slices. Halve, peel and thinly slice the red onion into small cubes. Wash and roughly chop the parsley, including the stalks

3. Grate the cheddar cheese block.

4. Wash the potatoes and cut them into 2cm cubes. Do not peel them.

5. Using a saucepan, add plenty of water and allow to reach boiling point. Add the potatoes to the boiling water, salt lightly and boil them until they are soft with a knife prick, roughly 15 to 20 minutes depending on the type of potato used.

6. Open the Foodi lid and place the sausages in the air crisp basket into the base of the cooking pot. Close the lid.

7. Select AIR CRISP and cook for 12 minutes. Check after 10 minutes that they are not burning.

8. Remove the sausages from the basket and move to a plate. Carefully slice the sausages into bite-sized chunks.

9. After the potatoes are cooked, remove from the heat and drain the saucepan.

10. Return the potatoes to the saucepan.

11. Add the mustard, the cheese and a small glug of milk. Season with salt and pepper. With the aid of a potato masher, mash the potatoes into a puree.

12. Open the Foodi lid and add a dessert spoon of olive oil to the cooking pot.

13. Select SEAR/SAUTÉ on the high setting and start it warming up. When the oil is warm, add the onion, carrot and cook for about 10 minutes. Stir regularly with a wooden, plastic or silicone spoon.

14. Add the flour and tomato puree/paste. Stir well and continue cooking for a further 2 minutes.

15. Add 250ml of water and the red wine stock pot. Again, stir very well. Allow to reach the boil.

16. After the sauce has reached the boil, use the TEMP

DOWN button until it says "LO" on the display. Allow the sauce to simmer while stirring until the sauce thickens, around 2 to 3 minutes.

17. Turn off the Foodi and add the sausage chunks and half of the chopped parsley. Mix in well.

18. With the aid of a non-metal implement such as a plastic spoon or fork, cover the sauce gently with the mashed potato, making sure that no sauce is visible from above. Spread well using the back of a fork to make an uneven surface that will crisp nicely when cooked.

19. Close the lid and select AIR CRISP. Cook for 10 minutes at 200°C

20. In the meantime, take a frying pan, turn on a medium heat and add the pancetta lardons or chopped bacon. No oil is needed.

21. Stir for 1 to 2 minutes until the lardons start to become golden. Add the chopped cabbage and a splash of cold water. Continue to fry, stirring well for 4 minutes or until the cabbage becomes tender.

22. Using a large plastic spoon or flat slice, plate up the pie and add the greens on the side. Enjoy.

DID YOU KNOW?

If you need to speed up the Sear/Sauté function, you can put the pressure lid onto the Foodi, switching the vent dial to VENT.

HOME-MADE PULLED PORK

INGREDIENTS

- 1kg of Pork shoulder
- 1 Onion
- 2 Garlic cloves
- 1 Bay leaf
- Olive oil
- 1 teaspoon Fennel seeds
- 4 sprigs of fresh Thyme or 4 teaspoons of dried
- 100ml of cheap White wine

Serves	3-4
Difficulty	●○○
Functions	Sear/Sauté Pressure
Time Prep	5
Time Cook	55

METHOD

1. Peel and finely dice the onion Peel and finely chop the garlic cloves. Add a tablespoon of oil to the cooking pot. Select SEAR/SAUTÉ using the high setting.

2. Season the pork well with salt and pepper and score slashes with a knife around the outside of the pork. Add the pork to the pot and cook for 5 minutes, turning occasionally to brown the outside. Remove the pork from the pot. Add 100ml of water and 100ml to the pot. Add the onion, fennel seeds, garlic, thyme and the bay leaf. Stir well for 5 minutes. Add the pork back into the pot. Fit the pressure lid.

3. Switch the vent dial to SEAL. Select PRESSURE and cook on high for 45 minutes. After the countdown timer has reached zero, allow it to count up to 4 minutes. Switch the vent dial to VENT and release the rest of the pressure. You should be able to easily shred the pork with two forks.

VEGGIE CURRY & HAKE

INGREDIENTS

- 2 Hake fillets
- 1 Pak choi
- 1 Carrot
- 400g of Potatoes
- 1 Spring onion
- Olive oil
- Salt & Pepper

Serves	2
Difficulty	●●○
Functions	**Sear/Sauté**
Time Prep	5
Time Cook	**35**

- 250ml of Coconut milk
- 4 dessert spoons of Plain flour
- 3 dessert spoons of Tikka Masala paste
- 1 Vegetable stock cube or vegetable OXO cube

METHOD

1. Boil a kettle with 200ml of water in it. Wash the potatoes. Chop unpeeled potatoes into 1cm cubes. Peel the carrot and cut into ½ cm wide slices.

2. Remove the roots from the spring onion and slice into fine rings. Keep the white and green parts of the spring onion separate from each other (the green parts will be used for decoration).

47

3. Wash the pak choi and remove the bottom ½ cm. Slice the pak choi horizontally into ½ cm wide strips.

4. Take a measuring jug and add 150ml of boiled water. Add the vegetable stock cube and stir until dissolved.

5. Open the lid of the Foodi and remove any accessories. Select SEAR/SAUTÉ using the high setting. Add 1 dessert spoon full of olive oil and allow to warm up fully. Add the potato cubes and cook for 3 minutes. Add the carrot slices and the white parts of the spring onion. Cook while stirring with a wooden spoon for a further 4 minutes.

6. Add the 3 dessert spoons of Tikka Masala paste, 250ml of coconut milk and the prepared vegetable stock. Cook for a further 13 minutes until the sauce has reduced and thickened. Add the pak choi and stir well.

7. In a deep plate, add 4 dessert spoons of plain flour, ¼ of a teaspoon of salt and some pepper. Stir well. Add the hake fillets and press them lightly until all parts of the fillets are coated in flour. For the last 8 minutes of the curry's cooking time, heat a frying pan on a medium heat, add a dessert spoon of olive oil. When the oil is hot, carefully add the fish and cook for between 6 and 7 minutes, flipping once half way through.

8. Divide the curry into 2 deep plates, add the fish on top and decorate with the green of the spring onion. Enjoy.

* DOUBLE THE INGREDIENTS TO SERVE MORE:

Due to the height of the side-walls of the cooking pot, and the fact that the sear/sauté function cooks from all sides, you can double the ingredients amount of all ingredients without needing to alter the cooking times at all.

CHUNKY HAM & PEPPER OMELETTE

INGREDIENTS

- ½ a Red pepper
- 8 Eggs
- 150ml Whole milk
- 4 or 5 slices of Ham
- Handful of fresh chives
- 100g of Grated Cheddar cheese
- Salt & Pepper

Serves	6
Difficulty	●●○
Functions	Bake/Roast
Time Prep	10
Time Cook	35

METHOD

1. Dice the red pepper after removing the seeds. Chop the chives into 2mm long tubes. Slice the ham into 1cm squares.

2. Remove any accessories. Pre-heat the Foodi by selecting BAKE/ROAST for 3 minutes.

3. In a mixing bowl, crack and add the eggs, the milk, salt and pepper and whisk well. Add the chives, grated cheese and ham. Grease the cooking pot base very well with margarine or cooking spray. Pour in the egg mixture.

4. Close the lid, select BAKE/ROAST and cook at 160°C for 30 minutes.

5. Use a wooden spoon, plastic fish slice or silicone spatula to slice and remove the thick omelette. Enjoy

HERBY PORK STEAKS WITH WEDGES & SALAD

INGREDIENTS

- 2 Pork loin steaks
- 600g of Potatoes
- A handful of Lettuce
- Some fresh chives
- 2 Tomatoes

Serves	2
Difficulty	●○○
Functions	**Air crisp**
Time Prep	5
Time Cook	30

- A few sprigs of Fresh tarragon or a teaspoon of ground tarragon
- 3 teaspoons of Red wine vinegar
- 2 teaspoons of Honey
- 40g of Butter
- 1 teaspoon of Wholemeal mustard
- 2 teaspoons of ground Paprika
- Salt & pepper to season
- Olive oil
- Rectangular (ideally) or rounded aluminium pie container

METHOD

1. Take the butter out of the refrigerator and allow to get to room temperature.

2. Remove lettuce leaves from the lettuce, wash and dry them and stack them on top of each other. Slice across them to make 1cm wide strips.

3. Halve the tomatoes and remove the green bits. Chop them into 1cm cubes.

4. Wash and slice the potatoes into 1 cm thick wedges. Put them into a bowl and add a dessert spoon of olive oil. Add 2 teaspoons of ground paprika and a little salt. Toss the wedges in the oil, paprika and salt until all are orange and oiled.

5. Open the Foodi lid and remove accessories from the cooking pot. If you have a foil pie container, fit it inside the foodi by shaping it as needed and putting it in upside down. Put the steaming rack with the horizontal part closed to the top, over the foil container to make it fit.

6. Remove the steaming rack and stack as many of the wedges onto the foil container as possible. Fit the steaming rack back in place and then carefully add the rest of the wedges around the base of the cooking pot.

7. Select AIR CRISP and cook at 180°C for 6 minutes.

Carry on with the preparation.

8. Cut the chives into small tubes. Pluck the tarragon leaves and chop them into tiny pieces. Take a small bowl and add the butter. If the butter is unsalted, add some salt. Add the tarragon and the chives and using a fork, stamp the herbs into the butter, mixing occasionally until a buttery paste is made.

9. Take a piece of greaseproof paper. Use a silicone spatula to scoop the butter into a rough sausage-like shape on the paper. Wrap the paper around the butter and shape it into a better sausage-like shape. Put this in the refrigerator until you are ready to serve.

10. Season the pork steaks with plenty of pepper and some salt.

11. When the wedges have stopped cooking, open the Foodi lid, give the wedges a little shove with a spoon to make sure that they're not sticking to the aluminium tray, add the pork loin steaks on top of the steaming rack and close the lid.

12. Select AIR CRISP and cook for 17 minutes at 180°C. Roughly half-way through the cooking time, open the lid and shove the wedges around a bit more and flip the pork steaks.

13. Take a large bowl and add 1 teaspoon of wholemeal mustard, 3 teaspoons of red wine vinegar (do not use malt vinegar), 2 teaspoons of honey, 1 tablespoon of olive oil and some salt and pepper. Stir it up well and add the tomato cubes and lettuce strips. Toss the salad well in the dressing. Remove the butter from the refrigerator and slice it into 1cm thick circles.

14. Plate-up the wedges and the pork loin steaks, add herbal butter on top of the pork and put a good handful of salad onto each plate. Enjoy.

PASTA BOLOGNESE

INGREDIENTS

- 1 Onion
- 2 cloves of Garlic
- 200g Fusilli pasta
- Olive oil
- Dried thyme
- 150g Mushrooms 400g Minced beef
- 2 cans of Chopped tomatoes
- 1 can of Baked beans (or Kidney beans plus a splash of water)
- 2 Beef OXO cubes or beef stock cubes
- Handful of cherry tomatoes

Serves	2-4
Difficulty	●●○
Functions	**Sear/Sauté Pressure**
Time Prep	**5**
Time Cook	**20**

METHOD

1. Boil a kettle with 400ml of water in it. Wash the mushrooms and slice into thin slices. Dice the onion. Open the cans of tomatoes and beans. If using kidney beans, drain using a sieve.

2. Open the Foodi and remove all accessories from the cooking pot. Add a small splash of olive oil.

3. Select SEAR/SAUTÉ using the high setting. When the pot is warm, add the beef mince, diced onion and break the mince apart using a wooden spoon.

4. When the beef mince is mostly cooked but not entirely, sprinkle a teaspoon of dried thyme and a pinch or two of salt into the pot and mix well.

5. Top with the pasta and pour both cans of chopped tomatoes over the ingredients.

6. Add the mushrooms and can of beans. If using kidney beans, add a splash of water. Do not stir the ingredients. Grate or crush the garlic cloves into the pot. Add the cherry tomatoes whole.

7. Crumble the OXO cubes over the ingredients and add 400ml of water around the sides of the cooking pot. If using beef stock cubes that are not OXO cubes, pour 200ml of boiling water into a measuring jug, mix in the beef stock cubes until they have dissolved and pour along the sides of the pot and not over the top.

8. Turn off the Foodi. Install the pressure lid. Switch the vent dial to SEAL. Select PRESSURE and pressure cook for 8 minutes on the high setting.

9. When the countdown timer has reached zero, let it count up for 1 minute (natural release). After a minute, switch the vent dial to VENT and allow the pressure to release quickly.

10. If liquid spurts from the vent, seal it again and allow pressure to naturally release again for a minute.

11. Repeat until all pressure has been released and the lid can be opened without effort. Mix well with a wooden spoon and serve. Enjoy.

FANCY FRENCH TOAST (V)

INGREDIENTS

- 6 medium-sized Eggs
- 4 slices of White bread
- A handful of Cranberries
- 1 teaspoon of ground Cinnamon
- ½ a tablespoon of Sugar
- Butter for greasing the cake tin

Serves	4
Difficulty	●○○
Functions	**Bake/Roast**
Time Prep	**5 + night**
Time Cook	**45**

METHOD

1. Grease a cake tin with butter, covering all parts inside the tin. Crack and beat all the eggs in a mixing bowl. Add the sugar, milk, cinnamon.

2. Pour the mixed ingredients into the cake tin. Add a handful of cranberries strewn around the mixture and then add the slices of bread, making sure that all slices are soaking up the egg mixture. Cover the tin either with a lid or clingfilm. Put in the refrigerator overnight.

3. When you're ready to cook, place the cake tin in the cooking pot and select BAKE/ROAST. Cook for 45 minutes at 180°C. Check in the last 10 minutes that the toast is not burning. Remove the cake tin and slice apart each slice of toast and serve. Enjoy.

SHEPHERD'S PIE

INGREDIENTS

- 2kg Potatoes
- 2 large Onions
- 2 Garlic cloves
- 500g Minced lamb
- Lamb stock (a lamb stock cube / pot in 500ml of boiling water)
- 120g Frozen peas
- HP/Daddies Brown sauce OR 1 tablespoon of Worcestershire sauce
- Tomato ketchup
- 3 Carrots or 150g frozen carrots
- 12 Button mushrooms (or a 200g punnet)
- Pinch of dried rosemary
- Pinch of dried thyme
- Pinch of dried parsley
- 2 tablespoons of plain flour
- 1 tablespoon of butter
- A glug of milk
- Olive oil
- Salt & Pepper

Serves	4-6
Difficulty	●●○
Functions	Grill Sear/Sauté Pressure
Time Prep	10
Time Cook	40

METHOD

1. Peel the potatoes and cut into bite-sized chunks

2. Place the air crisp basket into the cooking pot. Add 500ml of cold water to the cooking pot.

3. Fit the pressure lid, switch the vent dial to SEAL and select PRESSURE.

4. Pressure cook on high for 6 minutes. Due to the amount of water, this will take a while to reach pressure.

5. Quick release the pressure by switching the vent to VENT.

6. Remove the potatoes and put them into a bowl or saucepan for mashing.

7. In the empty cooking pot, without any accessory inside, add a dessert spoon full of olive oil and the finely chopped onions inside.

8. Peel and dice the carrots into cubes, add them to the pot.

9. Switch the Foodi on to SEAR/SAUTÉ on the high setting. Stir the pot contents and add the minced lamb. Use only wooden, silicone or plastic spoons to stir.

10. Keep stirring until all ingredients are well mixed. Cook for 8 to 9 minutes. Stir well every three minutes

11. After the meat and onions have browned, crush/press the garlic cloves into the cooking pot. Add the thinly chopped mushrooms, and stir in well.

12. Turn off the Foodi

13. Add 2 tablespoons of plain flour, the thyme, rosemary, parsley, a pinch of salt and pepper, a tablespoon of tomato ketchup, either 1 tablespoon of brown sauce or a tablespoon of Worcestershire sauce and stir in well until no flour can be seen.

14. Add the frozen peas to the top of the pot and then the lamb stock over the top slowly but do not stir from this point.

15. Install the pressure lid and switch the vent to SEAL.

16. Select PRESSURE and cook for 5 minutes using the

high setting.

17. Mash the potatoes in the bowl or saucepan, add a glug of milk and a spoonful of butter to aid mashing.

18. Switch the vent dial to VENT to release the pressure. If liquid starts to spurt through the vent, seal the vent again, intermittently releasing pressure until the lid may be removed.

19. Spoon the mashed potato over the top of the meat base and use a fork across the top of the mash layer to roughen it up a little.

20. Close the built-in lid and select GRILL. Grill the top of the shepherd's pie for 10 minutes until it has reached the desired level of crispiness.

21. Add a sprinkle of parmesan cheese if desired. Use only a plastic utensil to serve.

TIPS

To make it healthier, why not replace the potatoes with sweet potato?

To add a bit of colour to the insides, replace 120g of frozen peas with 40g peas, 40g frozen carrots and 40g frozen sweetcorn.

PIE & CHIPS FOR ONE

INGREDIENTS

■ Single shop-bought pie (for example Steak & Ale pie, Chicken & Mushroom pie etc)

■ Frozen chips

Serves	1
Difficulty	ooo
Functions	**Air crisp**
Time Prep	0
Time Cook	23

METHOD

1. Pre-heat the Foodi using the SEAR/SAUTÉ function for 3 minutes

2. Add the air crisp basket to the cooking pot and put enough frozen chips for one person in there, say two handfuls.

3. Close the built-in lid and select AIR CRISP at 180°C for 7 minutes

4. After the time is up, use a wooden spoon to create a gap in the centre and place a shop-bought defrosted pie, in its foil container, in that gap. Make sure all of the chips have also been moved around so that they do not stick to the bottom of the air crisp basket. Align the chips around the pie but not on top of it.

5. Select AIR CRISP again and cook at 160°C for 13 minutes, checking occasionally that the pie is not burning. Serve with boiled frozen peas and if suitable, gravy. Enjoy

CREAMY FETTUCCINI WITH CHICKEN & OYSTER MUSHROOMS

* INGREDIENTS

- 100g of Oyster mushrooms
- 2 Garlic cloves
- A bunch of Fresh chives

Serves	2-3
Difficulty	●●○
Functions	**Air crisp**
Time Prep	5
Time Cook	35

- 3 dessert spoons of Breadcrumbs
- 1 teaspoon of Chicken stock powder / 1 chicken stock cube or chicken OXO cube
- 250g of Fettuccini pasta (straight or as nests)
- 200g/200ml of Double cream
- A handful of fresh Parsley
- 2 tablespoons of Parmesan cheese
- 2 Chicken breast fillets or 250g of chopped chicken
- Salt & pepper to season
- Olive oil

METHOD

1. Boil a kettle with plenty of water in it.

2. Chop the chicken breasts into mouth-sized chunks.

3. Wash the oyster mushrooms and cut them into 1cm wide stripes.

4. Peel the garlic cloves.

5. Pluck the parsley from the stems and chop finely with a sharp knife.

6. Chop the chives into 2mm long tubes.

7. Take a measuring jug and add 50ml of boiling water. Add the chicken stock and stir until dissolved.

8. Pour plenty of boiling water into a saucepan, add salt and bring it to the boil. Add the fettuccini pasta nests to it and cook for about 12 minutes (check the cooking instructions from the packet).

9. Remove any accessories from the Foodi and select SEAR/SAUTÉ on the medium temperature setting. Add a dessert spoon of olive oil.

10. When the oil is hot, press one of the garlic cloves using a garlic press, keeping the other for later. Add the breadcrumbs and stir continuously for 2 minutes until the breadcrumbs are golden brown and very aromatic.

11. Carefully empty the cooking pot into a small bowl. Tip a quarter of the parmesan cheese into the small bowl and mix well.

12. Add another dessert spoon of olive oil to the cooking pot and increase the temperature to the high setting. When the oil is hot, add the chicken breast chunks and the mushrooms and cook for 4 minutes, occasionally stirring, until the chicken is no longer pink.

13. Add the cream and the measuring jug of chicken stock into the pot. Crush the remaining garlic clove into the pot and stir well. Cook for a further minute.

14. Add the rest of the parmesan cheese and season with salt and pepper. Turn off the Foodi.

15. After the fettuccini pasta has finished cooking, use a colander to drain it and throw it into the cooking pot.

16. Add the chopped parsley and fold everything in well and carefully, as the sauce is likely to splash and the parsley will stick to the bottom of the pot.

17. Divide the pasta and sauce onto 2 to 3 deep plates, sprinkling plenty of the prepared breadcrumbs on the top and decorate with the chopped chives. Enjoy.

TIPS

- If you cannot get your hands-on oyster mushrooms, due to their seasonal availability, use large button mushrooms sliced into quarters instead. If you slice them too small, they will easily break apart so keep the pieces large.

- Linguine pasta also works in place of fettuccini

* DOUBLE THE INGREDIENTS TO SERVE MORE:

Due to the height of the side-walls of the cooking pot, and the fact that the sear/sauté function cooks from all sides, you can double the ingredients amount of all ingredients without needing to alter the cooking times at all.

HOME-MADE TOMATO PASTA SAUCE

INGREDIENTS

- 5 large Tomatoes
- 1 large Carrot
- 3 Celery stalks
- 1/2 a Red pepper
- 2 Garlic cloves
- 1 Onion
- 1 Bay leaf
- 1 tablespoon of dried Goji berries
- 2 tablespoons of Butter
- ½ a Chicken stock cube or half a chicken OXO cube

Serves	4-6
Difficulty	●●○
Functions	Sear/Sauté Pressure
Time Prep	5
Time Cook	25

METHOD

1. Boil a kettle with at least 300ml of water in it.

2. Peel and cut the carrot.

3. Wash and chop the tomatoes.

4. Peel and dice the onion,

5. Chop the celery into thin half-moons.

6. Slice the pepper in half and remove the seeds. Chop into 1cm chunks.

7. Peel the garlic

8. Remove accessories from the cooking pot and add the butter. Select SEAR/SAUTÉ and use the high setting.

9. When the butter has melted, crush the garlic into the pot and add the onion. Stir well until the ingredients become very aromatic.

10. Add the carrot, tomatoes, celery and red pepper. Sauté further until the carrot has softened.

11. Pour in 250ml of boiling hot water.

12. Add the chicken stock cube, the bay leaf, goji berries and stir all together.

13. Fit the pressure lid, turning the vent dial to SEAL. Select PRESSURE. Pressure-cook for 15 minutes using the high setting.

14. When the countdown timer reaches zero, switch the vent dial to VENT and allow all the pressure to release quickly. Remove the lid

15. Transfer large amounts of the ingredients to a measuring jug, never more than half of the jug full at a time.

16. Use a hand-blender/mixer to reduce the mixture to a cream-like consistency. After blending, pour into a large saucepan and repeat until all of the ingredients in the cooking pot have been blended.

17. Season with salt and pepper.

18. Stir well and serve with pasta.

19. This recipe yields quite a lot of sauce so you may wish to use Tupperware or jars for home freezing.

VEGETARIAN LENTIL BAKE ⓥ

INGREDIENTS

- 2 Potatoes
- 1 Carrot
- ½ a Lemon
- 1 Garlic clove
- 1 Leek
- 380g of Brown lentils
- 1 dessert spoon of Yellow mustard
- ½ a dessert spoon of Tomato paste/puree
- 50g of Grated Cheddar cheese
- 200ml Whipping/double cream
- 1 small Sweet potato
- A handful of Fresh parsley
- ½ a head of Lettuce
- 3 dessert spoons of Soy sauce
- ½ a teaspoon of Ground nutmeg
- 1 tablespoon of Sunflower seeds
- 1 dessert spoon of Honey
- 1 Vegetable stock cube or vegetable OXO cube
- Olive oil
- Salt, Pepper & Sugar

Serves	2-3
Difficulty	●●○
Functions	Air crisp Sear/ Sauté Bake/Roast
Time Prep	5-10
Time Cook	50

METHOD

1. Cut the leek in half lengthways. Stack leek portions and wash thoroughly under the tap. Chop the leek into 1cm wide pieces.

2. Peel the carrot, potatoes and sweet potato. Slice each into ½ cm slices/rings.

3. Take a measuring jug and add 200ml of cream, ½ a teaspoon of ground nutmeg, 2 pinches of pepper and crumble the vegetable stock cube into it. Mix well with a fork.

4. Remove the stalks from the parsley and chop the leaves finely. Peel the garlic clove.

5. In a large bowl, add a dessert spoon of olive oil, salt and pepper. Add the vegetables and toss them well so all are coated in a little oil and seasoning.

6. Open the Foodi lid and put the air crisp basket in. Tip the vegetables into the basket and select AIR CRISP. Cook at 200°C for 10 minutes.

7. Half way through cooking, shake the basket to make sure nothing is stuck to the bottom or to other pieces.

8. When cooked, take the basket out of the Foodi and put onto an insulated surface for later.

9. Select SEAR/SAUTÉ on a medium-high setting. Add a dessert spoon of olive oil and let it warm up. Press the garlic clove into the cooking pot using a garlic press or grater. Cook for 2 minutes.

10. Add the lentils (without any liquid that may be in a carton/can) and ½ a dessert spoon of concentrated tomato puree/paste. Stir for a minute.

11. Add 3 dessert spoons of soy sauce, 1 dessert spoon of yellow mustard and ½ a teaspoon of sugar. Switch off the foodi and stir in the parsley.

12. Add half of the vegetables to the lentils and mix well. Then add the second half on top of the ingredients but this time do not mix them in, leave them layered.

13. Pour the cream mix from stage 3 all over the top.

14. Select BAKE/ROAST and cook for 30 minutes at 180°C. 5 minutes before the end of the baking time, open the lid and cover with grated cheddar cheese. Close the lid and let it continue to bake.

15. As the bake is cooking, wash the lettuce and rip into mouth sized pieces.

16. Slice the lemon into four quarters.

17. In a salad bowl, add 1 dessert spoon of honey, the juice from a lemon quarter, a dessert spoon of olive oil, a pinch of salt and pepper. Mix into a dressing. Add the lettuce and toss the salad well.

18. When the cooking has completed, use a plastic spoon to remove the bake from the Foodi in as few pieces as possible onto 2 or 3 plates.

19. Sit dressed salad next to it on each plate and garnish the salad with sunflower seeds. Add a lemon quarter to the edge of each plate. Enjoy.

DID YOU KNOW?

Some removable parts of the Ninja Foodi can be put into the dishwasher as normal cooking equipment. These are the cooking pot, air crisp basket, the vent dial from the pressure lid and the condensation container from the back of the device.

The pressure lid and seal must definitely not.

STICKY BAKED COD

INGREDIENTS

- 250g of Cod (2 fillets)
- 40ml or 3 tablespoons of Soy sauce
- 2 tablespoons of Honey

Serves	2
Difficulty	●○○
Functions	Bake/Roast
Time Prep	32
Time Cook	12

METHOD

1. In a deep plate or large bowl, add the soy sauce, the honey and 2 tablespoons of cold water. Mix it together well to form a sticky marinade and place the cod fillets into it.

2. Carefully turn the cod around in the marinade so that all parts are covered. Place the bowl into a refrigerator for 30 minutes to let the fish marinate.

3. Near the end of the marination time, put the steaming rack into the cooking pot with the horizontal platform closest to the bottom. Select BAKE/ROAST for 5 minutes at 180°C to pre-heat the device.

4. In a cake tin that fits comfortably onto the steaming rack, add the marinated fish and place the tin onto the steaming rack. Select BAKE/ROAST and cook for 12 minutes at 180°C

5. Carefully remove the tin from the Foodi and use a fish-slice to serve the fish.

6. Serve with fresh salad and boiled potatoes for a super healthy evening meal.

SMOKEY HADDOCK PARMENTIER

Better known in some regions as "Fisherman's Pie", this dish is perfect for cold winter evenings.

INGREDIENTS

- 400g of Carrots
- 750g of Potatoes
- 2 Garlic cloves
- 500g of Smoked haddock or fresh haddock
- 500ml of Whole milk
- A handful of fresh Parsley
- Grated Cheddar cheese (optional)
- Olive oil
- Pepper

Serves	4-5
Difficulty	●●○
Functions	Pressure Sear/Sauté Grill
Time Prep	5-10
Time Cook	25

METHOD

1. Take a bowl with some milk in it and add the smoked haddock to it. This will remove some of the saltiness of the fish. Keep it there until the recipe calls for it. Skip this stage if using fresh or frozen unsmoked haddock.

2. Peel and chop the potatoes into mouth-sized chunks. Peel and slice the carrots into 1cm thick rings. Peel the garlic cloves. Wash and chop the fresh parsley, excluding the stalks.

3. Remove any accessories from the cooking pot. Add the carrots, potatoes and garlic to the pot and add 200ml of cold water.

4. Install the pressure lid. Switch the vent dial to SEAL and select PRESSURE. Pressure-cook on the high setting for 7 minutes.

5. When the countdown timer has reached zero, switch the vent dial to VENT and allow all pressure to release.

6. Remove the lid. Empty the contents (with the aid of a sieve) without any remaining liquid into a large bowl for use later.

7. Add the smoked haddock into the pot and add 2 tablespoons of whole milk and 2 tablespoons of water.

8. Select SEAR/SAUTÉ and use the medium-high setting. Cook for 15 minutes.

9. Mash the vegetables in the bowl using a potato masher with a tablespoon and a half of whole milk, a tablespoon of olive oil, the chopped parsley and some pepper. Mash well.

10. After the haddock has finished cooking remove it from the pot and put it into a bowl. Remove any skin and bones from the haddock using a fork, mashing it well with the back of the fork.

11. Add the mashed haddock to the mashed vegetables and mix well.

12. Give the cooking pot a quick swill out and put it back into the Foodi. Select GRILL for 15 minutes. The first 5 minutes are to pre-heat the pot.

13. After the first 5 minutes add the mashed vegetables and fish, pat down a little and close the lid. Add some grated cheese to the top if you wish.

14. After the final 10 minutes of grilling, serve into deep plates. Enjoy.

THAI GREEN CHICKEN CURRY

INGREDIENTS

- 1 Courgette
- 1 Red pepper
- 100g Green beans
- 1 dessert spoon of Olive oil
- 1 teaspoon of Brown sugar
- 4 tablespoon of Thai green curry paste
- 400g Chicken breast
- 1 can of Coconut milk
- 1 tablespoon of Fish sauce
- 200ml Boiling hot water
- 1 Chicken stock cube / OXO cube
- Salt & Pepper

Serves	3-4
Difficulty	●●○
Functions	**Pressure Sear/Sauté**
Time Prep	**5-10**
Time Cook	**25**

METHOD

1. Prepare rice in a saucepan with a lid. (1 cup of rice to every 1 ½ cups of water, rinse the rice in a sieve, boil in the water. As soon as the rice has reached the boil, allow it to boil for 1 minute. Reduce the heat to the lowest setting and cover with a lid. Cook slowly without removing the lid for exactly 10 minutes. Turn off the heat and leave sealed closed for a further 12 minutes. Do not open the lid at any point and make sure the saucepan lid seals completely – ie, not a lid with a hole in it). As the rice is cooking, carry on with the recipe for the curry. Remove accessories from the Foodi

2. Cut the red pepper in half and remove the seeds. Slice length ways into strips and cut each strip into a few pieces. Dice the chicken breasts. Open the can of coconut milk

3. Cut the ends off the courgette, slice length ways and cut each courgette strip into thin half-moon slices.

4. If the green beans are fresh, wash them and remove the top and tail of them. Cut them into 3 pieces. (You can use frozen green beans).

5. Select SEAR/SAUTÉ and select HIGH. Press START/STOP and allow the pot to heat up for 3 minutes.

6. Add the oil and curry paste, salt & pepper and cook for 1 minute, stirring regularly. Add the chicken, coconut milk, water, chicken stock cube, fish sauce and brown sugar. Mix well.

7. Install the pressure lid. Switch the vent dial to SEAL Select PRESSURE and set to high and set the time to 5 minutes. Press START/STOP to begin.

8. When pressure cooking is complete and the countdown timer has reached zero, allow pressure to natural release for 2 minutes. After 2 minutes, quick release the remaining pressure by turning the vent seal to the VENT position. Remove the pressure lid. Select SEAR/SAUTÉ and select high temperature.

9. Add the courgette, red pepper and green beans. Cook for 4 minutes until the vegetables have softened a little but still retain a little crisp bite.

10. Open the rice saucepan lid and fluff-up the rice using a fork. Serve rice with the curry next to it.

BEEF-FRIED-RICE

INGREDIENTS

- 1 Red pepper
- 250g of Minced beef
- Soy sauce
- Brown sugar
- Honey
- 1 Lime
- 200g Jasmine / long-grain rice (1 cup)
- 1 chunk of fresh Ginger, thumb-sized.
- 1 Garlic clove
- 1 handful of fresh Coriander
- 150g Green beans (fresh or frozen)
- 250ml / 1 cup of cold water
- Salt & Pepper

Serves	2-4
Difficulty	●●○
Functions	**Pressure** **Sear/Sauté**
Time Prep	**5**
Time Cook	**30**

METHOD

1. Rinse the rice in a sieve under cold water until the water runs clear. Remove all accessories from the cooking pot. Add the rice to the cooking pot. Add 1 full cup of water (250ml) and ¼ teaspoon of salt. Fit the pressure cooker lid, turn the vent dial to SEAL Select PRESSURE and cook on high for 2 minutes.

2. Natural release (leave the vent in the SEAL position) for 10 minutes. Carry on with the preparation.

3. Top and tail the green beans if fresh, chop them into thirds. Halve the pepper and discard the core and seeds. Slice into thin strips. Zest and quarter the lime. Peel and grate the ginger. Peel and grate the garlic (or use a garlic press). Roughly chop the coriander (including the stalks and all).

4. Quick release (switch the vent to the VENT position). Scoop the rice out of the cooking pot into a large / deep bowl. Cover will clingfilm to keep moist. Quickly rinse out the cooking pot and return it to the Foodi. Select SEAR/SAUTÉ using the high setting. Add a glug of olive oil.

5. Add the mince and stir with a wooden spoon for 6 minutes (or until the mince is no longer pink). Spoon off any excess oil/fat and tip the mince over the rice, cover again with cling film.

6. Again, using the SEAR/SAUTÉ function on the high setting, add another glug of oil if the pot it not already oily. Add the pepper, green beans, a tablespoon of water. Stir well with a wooden spoon for 4 to 5 minutes. Stir the garlic and ginger into the pot. Cook for 1 minute.

7. Add two tablespoons of soy sauce, a teaspoon of brown sugar and a tablespoon of honey. Stir very well. Return the minced beef and rice to the pot and stir well until piping hot. Switch off the Foodi and stir in the lime zest, the juice from two lime quarters and half of the chopped coriander. Stir in.

8. Take two deep plates and put half of the ingredients in each. Scatter the rest of the coriander on top of each bowl and place a lime quarter on the side of each.

TIP

If you do not wish to use minced beef, substitute it with 2 skinless boneless chicken breasts, sliced into very thin strips.

SPICY CHICKEN NUGGETS

INGREDIENTS

- 1 Chicken breast per person (boneless & skinless chicken) – up to 3
- 1 Pack of spicy/chili Nachos or Doritos
- Egg, cracked and mixed for coating OR Mayonnaise
- 2 tablespoons of Flour
- Salt and Pepper
- Optional dip, such as:
  - Garlic sauce / Aioli sauce
  - Mango curry sauce
  - Sour cream
  - Sweet chili sauce
  - Honey and Mustard salad dressing

Serves	1-3
Difficulty	●●○
Functions	**Air crisp** **Sear/Sauté**
Time Prep	**5**
Time Cook	**15**

METHOD

1. Cut the chicken breasts into chicken nugget sized chunks

2. Put the nachos into a sandwich bag or equivalent, seal the bag with as little air as possible inside. Use a rolling pin to flatten the nachos into a-little-bigger-than-breadcrumbs consistency.

3. Get three deep bowls, put flour in one, egg, salt & pepper in another and the nachos crumbs in the final bowl.

4. Open the Foodi lid and pre-heat it using SEAR/SAUTÉ. Place the air crisp basket inside.

5. Carefully, take each chicken chunk, roll it in flour so that all surfaces are covered. With the aid of tongs, remove from the flour and dip in the egg. Then roll it slowly and carefully in the nacho crumbs. Finally, carefully place into the air crisp basket. Do not move it around.

6. Repeat the above until all chicken is coated and loosely stacked with some gaps between

7. Select AIR CRISP and cook at 200°C for 10 minutes, carefully turning them after 5 minutes, occasionally checking for burning.

8. Serve with dips or salad.

FISH FINGERS

INGREDIENTS

- Up to 10 Fish fingers

Serves	3-4
Difficulty	●○○
Functions	**Air crisp**
Time Prep	**0**
Time Cook	**12**

METHOD

1. Pre-heat the Foodi using the BAKE/ROAST function for 3 minutes

2. Add the fish fingers into the air crisp basket, put it in the Foodi and AIR CRISP at 180°C for 8 minutes, turning after 4 minutes.

FULL ENGLISH BREAKFAST

INGREDIENTS

- 6 rashers of Bacon
- 6 British or Irish sausages
- 2 Eggs
- ½ can of Heinz Baked Beans
- 2 Tomatoes
- 4 slices of Black Pudding
- 1 tablespoon of Butter, (softened or microwaved for 20 seconds)
- 2 dessert spoons of Milk
- Salt pinch
- Pepper pinch

Serves	3-4
Difficulty	●●○
Functions	**Air crisp**
Time Prep	**3**
Time Cook	**20**

METHOD

1. In a ramekin, silicone egg poacher or shallow oven-proof cup crack open two eggs. Add two dessert spoons of milk, a pinch of salt, a pinch of pepper and a teaspoon of softened butter. Mix the ingredients together using a fork until you cannot see the separate ingredients.

2. Add the air crisp basket to the cooking pot and add ramekin to it.

3. Slice the tomatoes in half and lightly salt. Stack them next to the ramekin two-by-two.

4. Surround the egg and tomatoes with bacon rashers, add sausages on top of the bacon. Add the black pudding wherever space may be found. The black pudding slices may be stacked vertically around the edges. Close the lid and select AIR CRISP. Cook for 10 minutes at 180°C. Half way through the cooking time, open the lid to stir the scrambled egg in the ramekin.

5. After the 10 minutes is up, remove the egg and add another ramekin or silicone egg poacher with half a can of beans in the available space. Cover the egg ramekin or poacher with aluminium foil to ensure it stays warm. Close the lid and air crisp for a further 5 minutes. If you wish, now is the time to add two slices of sliced bread to a toaster.

6. Remove all ingredients and plate up for two persons to enjoy.

JUMBO SAUSAGE ROLLS

INGREDIENTS

- 1, 2 or 3 Jumbo sausage rolls, frozen

Serves	1, 2 or 3
Difficulty	○○○
Functions	**Air crisp**
Time Prep	**0**
Time Cook	**16**

METHOD

1. Select BAKE/ROAST for 3 minutes to pre-heat the Foodi.

2. Place 1, 2 or 3 jumbo sausage rolls on the up-turned steam rack or in the air crisp basket

3. Select AIR CRISP and cook for 13 minutes at 180°C.

PRAWN LAKSA

INGREDIENTS

- 180g fresh or frozen King prawns
- 1 Lime
- 1 Red chili
- 200ml Coconut milk
- 2 tablespoons of Thai yellow curry paste (or 3 tablespoons of Thai green curry paste)
- 1 tablespoon of Peanut butter
- A 110g pack of dried Asian egg noodles
- Rainbow vegetable mix (which usually contain chunks of pak choi, baby corn, onion, broccoli & stalks, red pepper, carrot etc, or similar)
- 1 tablespoon of Soy sauce
- Salt, Pepper & Sugar
- Olive oil

Serves	2
Difficulty	●●○
Functions	**Sear/Sauté**
Time Prep	**5**
Time Cook	**10**

METHOD

4. Boil a kettle with 600ml of water in it. Halve the chili lengthways and remove the seeds using your knife. Chop finely. Zest the lime with a grater and cut into quarters.

5. Open the Foodi built-in lid, remove any accessories and drizzle a little olive oil into the cooking pot. Select SEAR/SAUTÉ on the high setting.

6. Add 2 tablespoons of Thai yellow curry paste (or 3 tablespoons of Thai green curry paste) and let it warm through. Add coconut milk, 550ml of boiling water, a tablespoon of peanut butter, half of the finely chopped red chili (the rest will be for decoration) and a pinch of sugar.

7. Stir all ingredients in well together.

8. Break up the egg noodles and add to the pot, cook for a minute on the low setting. Throw in the prawns and the vegetable mix, stir in carefully. The prawns are cooked when they are pink on the outside yet opaque in the middle.

9. After the prawns are cooked, stir-in the lime zest and a tablespoon of soy sauce. Squeeze two quarters of the lime as juice into the pot. Stir well. If the consistency seems too dry, add a splash of water. Some egg noodles absorb more liquid than others. The liquid should be the consistency of a thickened soup.

10. Season with a pinch of salt and some pepper. Divide the contents into two deep bowls and top with the remainder of the chopped chili. Place a lime quarter on the top side of each bowl. Enjoy… and be careful, it's quite spicy! If chili is too hot, swap with a spring onion. Cut into thin rings, added in stage 3 and keep some of the greener parts for decoration.

CHICKEN KORMA CRUMBLE

INGREDIENTS

- 300g of Chicken breast fillets (2 – 3 fillets)
- 1 Onion
- 2 Garlic cloves
- 1 Green chili
- 3 dessert spoons of Korma paste
- 200ml of Coconut milk
- 1 Chicken stock cube / chicken OXO cube
- 200g of Chickpeas
- A handful of Salted peanuts
- 25g Panko breadcrumbs
- A handful of Kale
- Salt & Pepper
- Olive oil

Serves	2-3
Difficulty	●●○
Functions	**Grill** **Sear/Sauté**
Time Prep	**5**
Time Cook	**30**

METHOD

1. Boil a kettle. Dice the chicken breasts. Slice into mouth-sized chunks.

2. Peel and dice the onion. Peel the garlic. Halve the chili lengthways and remove the seeds. Chop finely.

3. Drain and rinse the chickpeas using a sieve. Put half of the chickpeas into a bowl and the other half back in the carton for later.

4. Open the Foodi lid and remove any accessories. Select SEAR/SAUTÉ and use the high setting. Add a dessert spoon full of olive oil. When the oil is hot, add the chicken breast chunks, salt and pepper and stir well for a few minutes until the chicken is browned all around. Add the onion and cook for a further 4 minutes.

5. Add the korma paste, press the garlic cloves into the pot, add half of the chopped chili and mix well. Keep the rest of the chili for decoration. Cook for 1 minute

6. Pour the coconut milk into the pot, crumble the chicken stock cube in and add 200ml of water from the kettle. Add the chickpeas from the carton.

7. Use a fork to crush the chickpeas that have been put aside in a bowl until they form a paste. Add them to the pot and season with salt and pepper. Reduce the temperature of the SEAR/SAUTÉ program to low and allow to simmer for 8 minutes, stirring occasionally.

8. In a bowl, add the peanuts and roughly smash them with a back of a dessert spoon so that they are much smaller than usual. Add a tablespoon of olive oil and the panko breadcrumbs. Mix well together.

9. After the curry has thickened, stir in the chopped kale and allow it to simmer for a further 5 to 6 minutes. Again, season with salt and pepper if needed.

10. Carefully poor over the crumb mix from stage 8 and make sure most parts of the top of the curry are covered. Do not stir from now on. Close the built-in lid and select GRILL. Cook under the grill for 3 to 4 minutes until the crumb is golden brown.

11. Serve in 2 to 3 deep plates. Add the rest of the green chili as decoration to the top of each bowl. Enjoy.

HOME-MADE CHEESE BURGER & CHIPS WITH CREAMY MAYO DIP

INGREDIENTS

- 300g of Minced beef
- 2-3 teaspoons of Worcestershire sauce
- 1 Onion
- 3-4 Potatoes (400g)
- 25g of sliced Parmesan cheese

Serves	2-3
Difficulty	●●○
Functions	**Air crisp** **Sear/Sauté**
Time Prep	**10**
Time Cook	**45**

- Olive oil
- 1 beef Tomato
- 1 tablespoon of Paprika
- 2 Brioche buns
- Salt & Pepper
- 2 Wooden skewers to stabilize the burgers in their buns
- 4 slices of Lettuce
- 2 tablespoons of Natural yoghurt
- 1 tablespoon of Mayonnaise
- A few slices of Cheddar cheese

METHOD

1. Peel and dice the onion into very small pieces.

2. In a large bowl, add the minced beef, some salt, the finely diced onion and the Worcestershire sauce. Mix well together with your hands and form two equally-sized burger patties.

3. Open the Foodi and remove all accessories. Add a little oil to the base of the cooking pot and select SEAR/SAUTÉ on the medium-high setting. When the oil is hot, add the burger patties and cook for 7 full minutes, then flip and cook for a further 4 minutes.

4. Remove the burgers and place on some aluminium foil, wrap to keep warm. Quickly swill the cooking pot under a tap to remove the excess oil from the burgers.

5. Wash the 4 leaves of lettuce and spin to dry. Wash then slice the tomato into 2mm thick slices, removing the stem part. Ideally 3 slices per burger bun.

6. Wash the potatoes and peel them if you so wish. Slice the potatoes into French fry-sized chips, place them into a deep bowl.

7. Add a splash of sunflower oil, the paprika and some salt. Toss the chips well until all of them are oiled.

8. Add the chips to the air crisp basket and place the basket into the cooking pot.

9. Select AIR CRISP and cook the chips for 16 minutes at 180°C. Carry on with the recipe as the chips cook.

10. In a small bowl, mix the yoghurt, the mayonnaise and some salt and pepper to create a nice and tasty dip for the chips.

11. Slice the brioche buns in half and put them into the Foodi on top of the chips for 4 minutes, cut-side facing upwards. Remove them when they are nicely toasted.

12. Using a dessert spoon, spread a little of the dip from above onto the toasted side of the brioche buns. Add a slice of lettuce under the top part of each bun.

13. Divide the rest of the dip into 2 ramekins and serve onto the 2 plates.

14. When the timer has ended on the air crisping of the chips, remove the air crisp basket, put the burgers into the base air crisp basket, pushing the chips either on top of the burgers or stack the burgers on one side with the chips around them, both options work very well.

15. Select AIR CRISP and cook on 180°C for 5 minutes. After 4 minutes, add the cheese on top of the burgers.

16. Add the tomato slices on top of the lettuce. Open the Foodi lid and put each burger on top of the tomato slices then top each burger with slices of parmesan cheese.

17. Add the base of the brioche bun on top and use a wooden skewer to poke through the base of the bun to the top. Turn the brioche and burger over and surround with the chips. Enjoy.

DID YOU KNOW?

The Foodi is fitted with a short cable so that parents of young kids can be sure that their little ones cannot pull it from the worktop onto themselves.

For that reason, never use an extension cable with your Foodi.

COTTAGE PIE

INGREDIENTS

- 2kg Potatoes
- 2 large Onions
- 2 Garlic cloves
- 500g Minced beef
- Beef stock (a beef OXO cube / beef stock pot in 500ml of boiling water)
- 120g Frozen peas
- 1 tablespoon of HP/Daddies Brown sauce OR 1 tablespoon of Worcestershire sauce
- 1 tablespoon of Tomato ketchup
- 3 Carrots or 150g frozen carrots
- 12 Button mushrooms (or a 200g punnet)
- Pinch of dried rosemary
- Pinch of dried thyme
- Pinch of dried parsley
- 2 tablespoons of plain flour
- 1 tablespoon of butter
- A glug of milk
- Olive oil
- Salt
- Pepper

Serves	4-6
Difficulty	●●○
Functions	**Grill** **Pressure** **Sear/Sauté**
Time Prep	**10**
Time Cook	**40**

METHOD

1. Peel the potatoes and cut into bite-sized chunks

2. Place the air crisp basket into the cooking pot. Add 500ml of cold water to the cooking pot.

3. Fit the pressure lid, switch the vent dial to SEAL and select PRESSURE.

4. Pressure cook on high for 6 minutes. Due to the amount of water, this will take a while to reach pressure.

5. Quick release the pressure by switching the vent to VENT.

6. Remove the potatoes and put them into a bowl or saucepan for mashing.

7. In the empty cooking pot, without the air crisp basket inside, add a dessert spoon full of olive oil and the onions chopped finely.

8. Peel and dice the carrots into cubes, add them to the pot.

9. Switch the Foodi on to SEAR/SAUTÉ on the high setting. Stir the pot contents and add the minced beef. Use only wooden, silicone or plastic spoons to stir.

10. Keep stirring until all ingredients are well mixed. Cook for 8 to 9 minutes. Stir well every three minutes

11. After the meat and onions have browned, crush/press the garlic cloves into the cooking pot. Add the thinly chopped mushrooms, and stir in well.

12. Turn off the Foodi

13. Add 2 tablespoons of plain flour, the thyme, rosemary, parsley, a pinch of salt and pepper, 1 tablespoon of tomato ketchup, 1 tablespoon of either brown sauce or Worcestershire sauce and stir in well until no flour can be seen.

14. Add the frozen peas to the top of the pot and then the

prepared beef stock over the top slowly but do not stir from this point.

15. Install the pressure lid and switch the vent to SEAL.

16. Select PRESSURE and cook for 5 minutes using the high setting.

17. Mash the potatoes in the bowl or saucepan, add a glug of milk and a spoonful of butter to aid mashing.

18. Switch the vent dial to VENT to release the pressure. If liquid starts to spurt through the vent, seal the vent again, intermittently releasing pressure until the lid may be removed.

19. Spoon the mashed potato over the top of the meat base and use a fork across the top of the mash layer to roughen it up a little.

20. Close the built-in lid and select GRILL. Grill the top of the cottage pie for 10 minutes until it has reached the desired level of crispiness. Add a sprinkle of parmesan cheese if desired. Use only a plastic utensil to serve.

TIPS

To make it healthier, why not replace the potatoes with sweet potato?

To add a bit of colour to the insides, replace 120g of frozen peas with 40g peas, 40g frozen carrots and 40g frozen sweetcorn.

CHICKEN WINGS

INGREDIENTS

- 500g of small frozen chicken wings
- Optional barbecue sauce
- Seasoning as required

Serves	4
Difficulty	●○○
Functions	**Pressure** **Air crisp**
Time Prep	1
Time Cook	28

METHOD

1. Place the chicken wings in the air crisp basket of the Foodi and place the basket into the cooking pot.

2. Add 250ml of water to the base of the cooking pot.

3. Fit the pressure lid and switch the vent dial to SEAL

4. Select PRESSURE. Pressure cook on the high setting for 5 minutes. Yes, just 5 minutes.

5. Quick release pressure by switching the vent dial to VENT. When pressure has been fully released, remove the pressure lid.

6. Season with sea salt and cracked black pepper.

7. Close the built-in lid and select AIR CRISP. Cook for 15 to 20 minutes at 200°C, checking for burning after 8 minutes.

INDIAN VEGETARIAN TIKKA-MASALA WITH CHAPATI ⓥ

* INGREDIENTS

- 75 – 100g Baby spinach
- 250ml Coconut milk
- 1 large Red onion
- 40g or 3 dessert spoons of Tikka Masala paste

Serves	2
Difficulty	●●○
Functions	**Sear/Sauté**
Time Prep	**5**
Time Cook	**30**

- 1 very large sweet potato or 3 small-sized
- 400g Chopped tomato
- 4 tablespoons of Natural yoghurt (for vegetarian, Vegans can use more coconut milk)
- 2 Chapati bread (pre-cooked and ready to warm from the packet)
- Salt
- Pepper
- 2 teaspoons of Sugar
- Olive oil

METHOD

1. Peel the red onion and chop into 1/8s (chop into quarters and chop each quarter in half). Peel the sweet potato and chop into 2cm cubes. Open the Foodi lid and remove any accessories. Add 1 ½ dessert spoons of olive oil to the cooking pot

2. Select SEAR/SAUTÉ and allow it to warm up. Use the high setting. When the oil is hot, add the onion.

3. Stir well for 1 minute on the high setting before adding the sweet potato. Cook for a further 3 minutes while stirring with a silicone spatula or wooden spoon.

4. Reduce temperature to Medium-high and add the Tikka paste. Keep stirring for 1 minute. Add the chopped tomatoes and coconut milk. Add a pinch or two of salt and a teaspoon of sugar and continue to cook for 15 minutes. Stirring occasionally.

5. Turn on your oven to 200°C and put the chapati bread onto grease-proof paper in the oven as instructions for the chapati bread describe. The bread I had took only 5 minutes to warm through. At 11 minutes of the curry cooking time, add the baby spinach and carefully stir in well without splashing sauce everywhere.

6. Serve the curry into deep plates and fold a chapati bread onto the side of the plate. Add 2 tablespoons of yoghurt to the centre of the curry as decoration. Enjoy.

* DOUBLE THE INGREDIENTS TO SERVE MORE:

Due to the height of the side-walls of the cooking pot, and the fact that the sear/sauté function cooks from all sides, you can double the ingredients amount of all ingredients without needing to alter the cooking times at all.

COCA-COLA GAMMON JOINT

INGREDIENTS

- 1.3 – 1.5kg Gammon joint
- 1 litre of Coca-Cola
- Water

Serves	3-5
Difficulty	●●○
Functions	Pressure Sear/Sauté
Time Prep	1
Time Cook	65

METHOD

1. Boil a kettle with plenty of water in it. Remove all accessories from the Foodi. Place the gammon joint into the cooking pot and cover with boiling water.

2. Select SEAR/SAUTÉ and select the high setting. Allow the water in the pot to boil for 4 minutes.

3. Turn off the Foodi, remove the cooking pot carefully, take out the gammon and empty the water. Return the pot to the Foodi and put the gammon joint back in. Slowly add 1 litre of classic Coca-Cola to the pot. Do not use Diet Coke or Coke Zero., only use the classic version. The sugar content is essential.

4. Fit the pressure lid and turn the vent dial to SEAL. Select PRESSURE and cook on the high setting for 45 minutes. When the countdown timer reaches zero, allow the pressure to release naturally for 20 minutes. After 20 minutes, switch the vent dial to VENT. Remove the pressure lid when all pressure has released.

5. Remove the gammon from the pot, empty the water, insert the air crisp basket. Add the gammon again and AIR CRISP for 10 minutes at 200°C to glaze.

VIETNAMESE BEEF WITH CHILI-NOODLES & BEANS

INGREDIENTS

Serves	2-3
Difficulty	●●○
Functions	**Sear/Sauté**
Time Prep	**5**
Time Cook	**30**

- 1 Spring onion
- 1 Lemongrass
- 100g of Green beans
- 1 Red pepper (or yellow or orange but not green)
- 200g of Minced beef

- 1 Garlic clove
- 1 thumb-sized piece of Ginger
- 200g of Chili-noodles / linguine
- 1 ½ tablespoons of Soy sauce
- 1 dessert spoon of cornflour
- 1 Red chili
- 1 tablespoon of Hoisin sauce
- 1 Beef stock cube / beef OXO cube
- Olive oil
- 10g of Roasted peanuts

- Cracked black pepper
- Sea salt

Method

1. Boil a kettle. Wash and remove the ends of the green beans, cut into thirds.

2. Peel the garlic.

3. Remove the roots from the spring onion and slice fully into thin rings, keeping the white and green parts separate (green parts will be used for decoration).

4. Cut the pepper in half and remove the seeds. Chop into thin strips. Peel and grate the ginger into a bowl.

5. Halve the chili and remove the seeds. Cut into thin strips.

6. Take the lemongrass and put it flat on a chopping board. With the aid of a large kitchen knife, lay it flat upon the lemon grass and press with a lot of pressure down to squash the lemongrass. This releases the oil from inside the lemongrass. Do not cut the lemongrass.

7. Take a measuring jug and add 150ml of boiling water. Add the beef stock cube, the hoisin sauce and the cornflour. Mix very well together.

8. Take a large saucepan and fill it with plenty of boiling water. Add ¼ of a teaspoon of salt to it. Set to boil.

9. When boiling, add the chili noodles or linguine. Check the cooking instructions from the pasta regarding how long it should be cooked, minus 1 minute.

10. When cooked, pour them into a sieve or colander to drip dry. They do not need to be kept warm.

11. Open the Foodi lid and remove accessories. Switch the SEAR/SAUTÉ function to the high setting and add a dessert spoon of olive oil. When hot, add the minced beef. Break up with a wooden spoon and cook for about 2 minutes.

12. Add the pepper strips and cook for a further 3 minutes, stirring occasionally.

13. Add the white parts of the spring onion, the green beans and press the garlic clove using a garlic press.

14. Add the chili strips and the lemongrass on top (kink it slightly if it is too long) and add the grated ginger. Cook for 2 minutes until everything smells aromatic.

15. Add the measuring jug contents and stir in well. Season with salt and pepper.

16. When the pasta is cooked and drained, throw it into the pot and mix well. Add salt and pepper as required. Remove the lemongrass.

17. Serve into 2 or 3 deep plates/bowls, sprinkle peanuts onto all portions and decorate with the green spring onion rings and any remaining chili strips.

18. Add the soy sauce to the table for those who wish for a stronger flavour. Enjoy.

DID YOU KNOW?

When using the air crisp function, it's better to have the ingredients roughly the same size for even cooking

CHICKEN TIKKA-MASALA CURRY WITH CHICKPEAS

* INGREDIENTS

- 1 small Sweet potato
- 250ml Coconut milk
- 1 Onion
- 1 large Potato
- 1 Courgette

Serves	2-3
Difficulty	●●○
Functions	**Air crisp** **Sear/Sauté**
Time Prep	5
Time Cook	45

- 2 Chicken breast fillets
- 1 teaspoon of Vegetable stock / 1 vegetable stock cube or a vegetable OXO cube
- 1 Spring onion
- 2-3 dessert spoons of Tikka-masala paste (depends on how spicy you want it!)
- 150g - 200g Chickpeas (a carton)
- Salt & Pepper
- Olive oil
- 100ml of boiling water for the stock.

METHOD

1. Boil a kettle with a glass of water in it.

2. Peel the potato and the sweet potato. Dice into 1cm cubes.

3. Cut the ends off the courgette and cut lengthways into quarters. Cut through all four parts to make 1cm large chunks.

4. Add the vegetables to a large bowl and add a dessert spoon full of olive oil, salt and pepper and toss well together.

5. Open the Foodi, insert the air crisp basket and add the oiled vegetables to it. Select AIR CRISP and cook at 200°C for 15 minutes. Carry on with the recipe while the vegetables are cooking.

6. Check in the last few minutes that the vegetables are not burning. Remove the air crisp basket from the cooking pot.

7. Cut the roots from the spring onion and slice into thin rings. Keep to the side for decoration purposes.

8. Drain the carton of chickpeas and quickly run under a tap using a sieve until the water runs clear.

9. Take a measuring jug and add 100ml of boiling water. Add the vegetable stock and stir until dissolved.

10. Chop the chicken breast fillets into mouth-sized chunks. Peel the onion and slice into very thin slices.

11. Open the Foodi lid and add 1 dessert spoon of olive oil to the cooking pot. Select SEAR/SAUTÉ using the high setting. Add the chicken breast, the onion and stir them around for 3 to 4 minutes.

12. Reduce the temperature a little to the medium setting. Add the tikka-masala paste and stir it well for 1 minute.

13. Add the prepared vegetable stock and keep stirring. Let it cook for 5 minutes.

14. Add the coconut milk and the chickpeas to the sauce and stir once, letting the pot cook for 5 to 7 minutes until you reach the desired sauce thickness or consistency.

15. Add the vegetables from the air crisp basket to the sauce and let it warm up a little.

16. Season with salt and pepper. Serve the sauce into 2 or 3 deep plates and decorate with the spring onion rings. Enjoy.

* DOUBLE THE INGREDIENTS TO SERVE MORE:

Due to the height of the side-walls of the cooking pot, and the fact that the sear/sauté function cooks from all sides, you can double the ingredients amount of all ingredients without needing to alter the cooking times at all.

DID YOU KNOW?

You can speed up most sauté processes by putting a lid onto the Foodi… just not the supplied lids.

Most large frying pans are 28cm in diameter, so a lid that fits your frying pan probably fits the Foodi

VEGETARIAN ASIAN NOODLE STIR-FRY WITH LEMONGRASS Ⓥ

INGREDIENTS

Serves	2-3
Difficulty	●●○
Functions	**Sear/Sauté**
Time Prep	**5**
Time Cook	**30**

- 1 Spring onion
- 1 Lemongrass
- 2 Red pepper

- 150g of Mushrooms
- 1 Garlic clove
- 15g of fresh Ginger / roughly thumb-sized
- 200g of Chili-noodles / linguine
- 1 ½ tablespoons of Soy sauce
- 1 dessert spoon of Sesame seeds
- 1 Red chili
- 250ml Coconut milk
- 1 tablespoon of Sesame oil

- Olive oil
- Sugar
- Cracked black pepper & Sea salt

METHOD

1. Boil a kettle

2. Peel the garlic. Remove the roots from the spring onion and slice fully into thin rings, keeping the white and green parts separate (green parts will be used for decoration).

3. Cut the pepper in half and remove the seeds. Chop into thin strips.

4. Wash the mushrooms and slice into very thin slices. Peel the ginger and grate it into a bowl.

5. Halve the chili and remove the seeds. Cut into thin strips.

6. Take the lemongrass and put it flat on a chopping board. With the aid of a large kitchen knife, lay it flat upon the lemon grass and press with a lot of pressure down to squash the lemongrass. This releases the oil from inside the lemongrass. Do not cut the lemongrass.

7. Take a large saucepan and fill it with plenty of boiling water. Add ¼ of a teaspoon of salt to it. Set to boil. When boiling, add the chili noodles or linguine. Check the cooking instructions from the pasta regarding how long it should be cooked, minus 1 minute.

8. When cooked, pour the noodles or pasta into a sieve or colander to drip dry. They do not need to be kept warm.

9. Open the Foodi lid and remove accessories. Add the sesame seeds to the pot without oil and cook them for 2 minutes on the SEAR/SAUTÉ function on the high setting.

10. When browned or the aroma is noticed, carefully tip them into a bowl for later use (decoration).

11. Switch the SEAR/SAUTÉ function to the medium setting and add the sesame oil. When hot, add the white parts of the spring onion and press the garlic clove using a garlic press.

12. Add the lemongrass on top (kink it slightly if it is too long) and add the grated ginger. Cook for 1 to 2 minutes until everything smells aromatic.

13. Add the pepper strips and the mushroom slices. Cook for 4 minutes. Add the soy sauce, the coconut milk and a teaspoon of sugar.

14. When the pasta is cooked and drained, throw it into the pot and mix well. Add salt and pepper as required. Remove the lemongrass.

15. Serve into 2 or 3 deep plates/bowls, sprinkle sesame seeds onto all portions and decorate with the green spring onion rings and chili strips. Enjoy.

DID YOU KNOW?

It is possible to remove the X-shaped feet (the diffuser) from the air crisp basket for cleaning. Be ultra-careful when removing it because they are prone to snapping. Replacements can be bought via the NinjaKitchen.co.uk website, although they frequently "sell-out". Google search for "Replacement diffuser Nina Foodi OP300UK", for example.

CHEESY BEEF & POTATO JUMBLE

INGREDIENTS

- 1kg Minced beef
- 8 medium-sized Potatoes or 5-6 large potatoes
- 1 Onion
- 2 Garlic cloves
- 180ml Cream
- 1 Beef stock cube or beef OXO
- 250g Grated Cheddar cheese
- 250ml Boiling water

Serves	4-6
Difficulty	●●○
Functions	Sear/Sauté Pressure Air crisp
Time Prep	5
Time Cook	40

METHOD

1. Open the Foodi and remove all accessories

2. Finely dice 1 onion. Crush 2 garlic cloves into a bowl. Select SEAR/SAUTÉ on the high setting. Add the beef mince, garlic and onion to the cooking pot and stir well as the pot warms up. Brown the mince thoroughly. Turn off the Foodi.

3. Peel 8 potatoes and cut into mouth sized chunks. Add the potatoes on top of the beef. Crumble the beef stock cube over the potatoes and pour in 250ml of boiling water from the kettle.

4. Fit the pressure lid. Switch the vent to SEAL. Select PRESSURE and pressure cook for 10 minutes on the high setting.

5. Quick release pressure by switching the vent to VENT. Remove the lid.

6. Season with salt and pepper. Stir-in the 180ml of cream and only 150g of grated Cheddar cheese (keeping 100g for the topping later) carefully using a wooden spoon and slowly so as not to destroy the softened potatoes.

7. Close the built-in lid and select AIR CRISP. Cook at 200°C for 10 minutes.

8. Open the lid, stir the mix well, close the lid and air crisp for a further 5 minutes. Open the lid, stir the mix well and add the remaining 100g of Cheddar cheese to the top, spread evenly. Do not stir from now on.

9. Close the lid again and air crisp for a further five minutes, checking regularly. When the cheese is bubbling away, you're ready to serve. Use a wooden spoon or plastic slice to serve. It will not look pretty but it will taste incredible.

10. Garnish with some chopped chives and serve with boiled vegetables on the side.

DID YOU KNOW?

When baking cakes or something that requires an all-round heat to cook, choose a black or very dark coloured tin or pan to cook in. The blacker the surface colour of the pan, the quicker it will absorb heat and therefore the quicker your food will cook. Use a silver coloured tin or pan to reflect some of the heat away from the sides such as for baking a dense bread.

SPICY BEEF CURRY WITH RICE

- 2 tablespoons of Sunflower oil
- 500g of beef (stewing or braising steak)
- 1 tablespoon of Butter
- 1 large Onion
- 2 Garlic cloves
- 1 thumb-sized piece Ginger
- ¼ teaspoon of Chili powder
- 1 teaspoon of Turmeric
- 2 teaspoon of Ground coriander
- 3 Cardamom pods
- 400g of Chopped tomatoes
- 500ml of boiling water
- 1 Beef stock cube or beef OXO cube
- 1 teaspoon of Sugar
- 2 teaspoons of Garam masala powder
- 2 tablespoons of Double cream (optional)
- ½ a small bunch of fresh Coriander
- Naan bread and long-grain rice (*), to serve

Serves	4
Difficulty	●●○
Functions	Sear/Sauté Pressure
Time Prep	10
Time Cook	35

METHOD

1. Peel and finely chop the onion. Peel the garlic. Crush 3 cardamom pods, wash and roughly chop the coriander. Peel and grate the ginger.

2. Crush the garlic into a small bowl.

3. Remove accessories from the cooking pot. Select the SEAR/SAUTÉ function using the high setting. Add a tablespoon of sunflower oil and let it get hot.

4. Add the steak/beef and brown the outsides of the meat, constantly turning. Remove and set aside into a bowl.

5. Add the rest of the oil and add the butter, allow the butter to melt in the pot.

6. Add the onion and allow it to caramelise and brown off. This can take up to 8 minutes.

7. Add the ginger, garlic, turmeric, chili, dried coriander and cardamom. Stir well and cook for 2 minutes.

8. Add the beef, stirring well to coat the meat. Add 500ml of boiling water, the stock cube, the chopped tomatoes, cream, garam masala and the sugar. Stir well and cook for a further 10 minutes using the medium temperature setting.

9. *** Optional part of the recipe**: insert the steaming rack with the flat part nearest the top of the cooking pot. In a cake tin or metal pie case, tip a cup of rice in and add slightly more than 250ml of water. If this fits without spilling, add this on top of the steaming rack in the foodi.

10. Fit the pressure lid. Turn the vent dial to SEAL. Select PRESSURE and the high setting. Cook for 7 minutes.

11. After the countdown timer has reached zero, allow the timer to count up to 10 full minutes, this is a natural release.

12. After the 10 minutes is up, you may switch the vent dial to VENT to release any further pressure.

13. Serve into 4 deep plates and decorate with the fresh coriander. Enjoy.

FISH IN CRISPS

INGREDIENTS

- 4 or 5 fresh or frozen fillets of Fish (Cod, haddock, pollock)
- 180g of Plain flour
- A large bag or 2 small bags of salt and vinegar crisps
- 2 Eggs
- Salt

Serves	4-5
Difficulty	●●○
Functions	**Air crisp**
Time Prep	15
Time Cook	10

METHOD

1. Arrange 3 deep plates on the worktop. Open the bag(s) of crisps and flatten with the aid of a rolling pin. The crisp crumbs go in one bowl.

2. Crack the eggs into the second plate/bowl and mix them up with a fork.

3. Add the flour into the final plate/bowl and add half a teaspoon salt. Mix well.

4. Take each fish fillet and first roll them in flour, then in egg and finally in the crisps.

5. Repeat until all parts of all fish fillets are coated.

6. If you have time, or if you have read ahead, place the final plate/bowl of crisp-coated fish fillets into the refrigerator for half an hour to keep cool and firm up.

7. Remove from the refrigerator and spray them lightly with oil. Add the air crisp basket to the cooking pot and carefully add the fish to it. Do not stack the fish.

8. Select AIR CRISP.

9. Cook on air crisp for 10 minutes at 200°C. Serve with chips, of course! Enjoy.

CHEESE & HAM OMELETTE

INGREDIENTS

- 4 Eggs
- Butter for greasing
- 4 slices of Ham
- Salt & Pepper
- 60g of Grated Cheddar cheese

Serves	2
Difficulty	●○○
Functions	**Bake/Roast**
Time Prep	1
Time Cook	25

METHOD

1. Chop the ham slices. Select BAKE/ROAST at 190°C for 3 minutes to pre-heat. Grease a cake tin thoroughly with butter, leaving no part un-greased.

2. In a bowl, whisk all 4 eggs then add the cheese, salt, pepper and half of the chopped ham. Pour the mixture into the cake tin.

3. Throw in the rest of the chopped ham.

4. Place the cake tin into the empty cooking pot.

5. Select BAKE/ROAST and cook at 190°C for 20 minutes.

6. Check the omelette in the last few minutes that it is not burning.

7. Serve and enjoy.

TIP

A 3-egg version can be cooked using AIR CRISP at 200°C for just 10 minutes. Again, use the cake tin but put the cake tin on the steaming rack.

DID YOU KNOW?

If you have food to reheat but don't want it to burn and need it to retain its moisture, use the STEAM function for about 5 minutes. Don't forget to add at least 250ml of hot water to the bottom first, as well as switching the vent dial to VENT.

SATAY VEGGIE CHILI-NOODLES Ⓥ

INGREDIENTS

- 3 Carrots
- 1 Spring onion
- 15g Peanuts
- 1 Red chili
- 2 tablespoons of Soy sauce

Serves	2-3
Difficulty	●●○
Functions	**Sear/Sauté**
Time Prep	**5**
Time Cook	**30**

- 1 Lime
- 170g Sugar-snap peas / mange tout
- 8g or half of a thumb of Fresh ginger
- 2 Garlic cloves
- 200g of Chili-noodles or linguine
- 150ml of Coconut milk
- 4 dessert spoons of Peanut butter
- Salt & Pepper
- Olive oil

METHOD

1. Boil a kettle. Peel the garlic. Remove the roots from the spring onion and slice fully into thin rings, keeping the white and green parts separate (green parts will be used for decoration). Peel and cut the carrot into strips. Wash the mange tout / sugar-snap peas, remove any stems and cut each in half. Peel the ginger and grate it into a bowl. Halve the chili and remove the seeds. Cut into thin strips.

2. In a large bowl, add the sugar-snap peas / mange tout and cover in boiling water from the kettle. Allow to sit and soften.

3. Take a large saucepan and fill it with plenty of boiling water. Add ¼ of a teaspoon of salt to it. Set to boil. When boiling, add the chili noodles or linguine. Check the cooking instructions from the pasta regarding how long it should be cooked, minus 1 minute. When cooked, pour the noodles or pasta into a sieve or colander to drip dry. They do not need to be kept warm.

4. Open the Foodi lid and remove accessories. Select the SEAR/SAUTÉ function to the medium setting and add a dessert spoon of olive oil.

5. When hot, add the white parts of the spring onion and press the garlic cloves using a garlic press.

6. Add the chili on top and add the grated ginger. Cook for 1 to 2 minutes until everything smells aromatic.

7. Add the sugar-snap peas / mange tout and carrot slices. Cook for 2 minutes. Add half of the soy sauce (only 1 tablespoon here), the coconut milk and cook for 3 to 5 minutes.Slice the lime into four quarters.

8. Pour the vegetables out of the cooking pot into a deep bowl and cover in a large plate to keep warm. The pot does not need to be washed.

9. In the cooking pot on the SEAR/SAUTÉ setting on medium temperature, add the rest of the soy sauce (1 tablespoon), coconut milk, 50ml of boiling water and the peanut butter. Stir really well to make a thick sauce.

10. Add salt, pepper and the juice of a lime quarter. Add the vegetables back into the pot and stir well. When the pasta is cooked and drained, throw it into the pot and mix well.

11. Serve into 2 or 3 deep plates/bowls, sprinkle peanuts onto all portions and decorate with the green spring onion rings and a lime quarter. Enjoy.

CHICKEN NUGGETS & CHIPS

INGREDIENTS

- Chicken nuggets
- Frozen chips

Serves	2-4
Difficulty	ооо
Functions	Bake/Roast Air crisp
Time Prep	0
Time Cook	23

METHOD

1. Open the lid of the Foodi and insert the air crisp basket inside. Select BAKE/ROAST for 3 minutes at 180°C

2. After the pre-heat has completed simply pour in as many frozen chips as you need and as many chicken nuggets too. Plate them up frozen first to measure out, empty them into the basket and close the lid.

3. Select AIR CRISP and cook for 20 minutes at 180°C. After 10 minutes, give the basket a little shake to loosen any ingredients that may be stuck together or not been exposed to the full heat. Enjoy.

BRATWURST WITH PASTA SALAD

INGREDIENTS

- 250g of Penne pasta
- 150g Cherry tomatoes
- 100g / 100ml of Natural yoghurt
- 2 tablespoons of Mayonnaise

Serves	2
Difficulty	●○○
Functions	Sear/Sauté
Time Prep	5
Time Cook	35

- 1 tablespoon of Pesto
- 1 Cucumber
- 2 German bratwurst sausages *(Aldi, Lidl, Tesco)*
- 20g or 1 ½ tablespoons of Parmesan cheese flakes
- A handful of fresh Chives
- 80g of Bacon lardons / Pancetta lardons
- Salt & Pepper
- Olive oil

METHOD

1. Boil the kettle. Take a large saucepan and pour at least half a litre of boiling water into it. Add some salt.

2. Add the penne pasta and stir occasionally so not to stick to the pan. Carry on with the recipe as the pasta cooks.

3. Chop the tomatoes in halves.

4. Cut the ends off the cucumber and slice it lengthways in half. Slice half-moon-shaped 1cm thick slices.

5. Cut the chives into short tubes.

6. Take a large bowl and add the yoghurt, the pesto, the mayonnaise. Stir well to make a dressing. Season with salt and pepper.

7. Add the cucumber, the tomatoes and half of the chopped chives. Toss the salad well.

8. Open the Foodi lid and remove any accessories. Select SEAR/SAUTÉ using the medium setting.

9. When the pot is hot, add the bacon or pancetta. Stir well to break apart the cubes. Sauté for about 6 minutes until they are browned and crispy.

10. After the pasta is cooked, according to the cooking instructions, drain well using a sieve, run it under a cold tap to cool and then throw the pasta into the salad.

11. Add the bacon or pancetta.

12. In the base of the cooking pot, sauté the sausages for around 8 minutes, rotating often, until they are nicely browned.

13. Serve the pasta salad onto deep plates, cover with chives and place the sausage on the top. Sprinkle with parmesan flakes and enjoy.

SUNDAY ROAST BEEF

INGREDIENTS

- 500-750g Beef roasting joint
- 1 teaspoon of Beef stock powder or 1 beef stock cube

Serves	3-4
Difficulty	●○○
Functions	**Pressure Air crisp**
Time Prep	**1**
Time Cook	**35**

METHOD

1. Boil a kettle with at least 500ml of water in it. Remove all accessories from the cooking pot and pour 500ml of boiling water into it. Add the beef stock and stir with a wooden spoon until dissolved. Add the beef joint to the pot, sitting in the water.

2. Install the pressure lid and switch the vent dial to SEAL. Select PRESSURE and pressure cook for 15 minutes (to be still pink inside) using the high setting. When the countdown timer has reached zero, allow the timer to reach 5 minutes, then switch the vent dial to VENT to release the pressure before removing the lid.

3. Take the beef out of the pot, tip the liquid in the base into a jug to use with making a gravy later and put the air crisp basket into the pot. Put the beef into the pot and select AIR CRISP. Cook for 7 minutes at 200°C.

4. When the beef is cooked, check with a meat thermometer to check that it is cooked as required. Without resting the meat, the beef will be 40°C inside for rare, 48°C for medium and above 50°C for well done.

5. Wrap the beef in aluminium foil and allow it to rest for 10-20 minutes before carving and serving.

HAND-MADE TURKISH KEBAB MEAT

INGREDIENTS

- 750g of Minced beef
- 2 teaspoons of Cumin
- 2 teaspoons of dried Coriander or 8g of fresh coriander
- 2 teaspoons of Salt
- 1 teaspoon of dried Oregano
- ½ a teaspoon of Cracked black pepper
- 1 teaspoon of dried Garlic powder
- 1 teaspoon of Chili powder
- 1 teaspoon of Paprika
- 1 teaspoon of dried Onion powder (optional)
- Aluminium foil for wrapping and cooking

Serves	3-4
Difficulty	●●○
Functions	**Pressure**
Time Prep	10
Time Cook	40

METHOD

1. Add the minced beef into a large mixing bowl. Add the onion powder, garlic powder, cumin, coriander, salt, oregano, pepper, chili and paprika to the bowl and mix really well.

2. Kneed everything really well together, pressing it through your fingers until the separate ingredients can no longer be seen.

3. Form a large, wide sausage shape no longer than the width of the Foodi cooking pot.

4. Take a long piece of aluminium foil and wrap the sausage shape really tightly, screwing the top and bottom ends together equally tightly.

5. Open the foodi lid and place the steaming rack with the flat base closest to the bottom. Place the foil-wrapped meat onto the rack.

6. Add 500ml of water to the base of the cooking pot.

7. Install the pressure lid and switch the vent dial to the SEAL setting.

8. Select PRESSURE and cook on the high setting for 30 minutes

9. After the countdown timer reached zero, switch the vent dial to VENT to release the pressure. Remove the lid

10. Take out the steaming rack, empty the cooking pot of any water and put it back into the cooking pot. Unwrap the foil of the meat and carefully transfer it onto the steaming rack.

11. Select AIR CRISP and cook at 180°C for 5 minutes. After a few minutes, check and if the meat is being evenly cooked and if necessary, turn it around slightly, close the lid and continue to cook.

12. Remove the meat and place on a large plate. Use a skewer in the end of the meat to hold it firmly and use a sharp straight knife along the long edges of the meat to slice very thin slices, rotating after each slice is made.

13. You can return the meat without the skewer to the foodi if you wish to air crisp further for the next slices.

CHICKEN SCHNITZEL & POTATOES

INGREDIENTS

- Sunflower oil
- 400g of baby Potatoes
- 1 large Egg
- 2 Chicken breasts
- 1 tablespoon of Dijon mustard

Serves	2
Difficulty	●●○
Functions	**Air crisp** **Bake/Roast**
Time Prep	**25**
Time Cook	**12**

- 40g of Panko breadcrumbs
- 2 tablespoons of Plain flour
- A side salad or a slice of lemon (optional)

METHOD

1. Wash the potatoes and peel them if you so wish. Slice the potatoes in half, place them into a deep bowl. Add a splash of sunflower oil and some salt. Toss the potatoes well until all of them are oiled. Add to the air crisp basket and place the basket into the cooking pot. Select AIR CRISP, cook the potatoes for 15 minutes at 180°C.

Carry on with the recipe as the potatoes cook.

2. Butterfly-slice each chicken breast so that a flat piece of chicken results. Flatten further with a meat tenderizer if you have one. Otherwise, place a small piece of greaseproof paper on top of the chicken and bash it firmly until it is wider and flatter.

3. Take 3 deep plates. In one, add the flour with some salt and pepper. In another, add the Dijon mustard and the egg, mix it up. In the final plate, add the breadcrumbs.

4. Take each chicken piece, press it into the flour so that all is covered. Then transfer it to the egg, covering it completely in egg. Then transfer it to the breadcrumbs, ensuring all parts of the chicken is breaded. Transfer each chicken piece finally to a large plate until you are ready to use it.

5. When the potatoes have reached the end of the cooking time, pour them out into the cooking pot. Place the steaming rack into the cooking pot, with the horizontal shelf of the rack closest to the lid, being careful as to not squash the potatoes. There should be enough space for both schnitzels to fit on the rack without overlapping.

6. Close the built-in lid. Select BAKE/ROAST and bake on 180°C for 10 minutes. After 5 minutes, turn each schnitzel over, being careful not to damage the breaded layer as you turn them. Close the lid to continue cooking.

7. Open the lid and carefully remove the steaming rack. Check that the potatoes are cooked. Serve the schnitzel onto two plates, add the potatoes and a slice of lemon.

SWEET CHILI SALMON FILETS

INGREDIENTS

- 2 or 3 frozen Salmon filets
- Olive oil
- 2-3 tablespoons of Sweet chili sauce

Serves	2-3
Difficulty	●○○
Functions	**Air crisp**
Time Prep	1
Time Cook	23

METHOD

1. Defrost 2 or 3 salmon filets naturally (do not use a microwave to defrost or use a hot water method, the salmon will become fragile).

2. Take a foil pie container or a cake tin and spray lightly with oil. Wipe the oil across the base of the tin/container using a piece of grease-proof paper such that all parts of the base are covered. Place the salmon filets into the tin/container and smear the tops liberally with sweet chili sauce. Turn over and repeat so that all parts of the salmon filets are covered liberally in sweet chili sauce.

3. Place the steaming rack in the cooking pot with the horizontal part of the rack closest to the bottom of the pot. Carefully stack the cake tin or pie container onto the rack and close the built-in lid.

4. Select AIR CRISP and cook the salmon filets for 23 minutes at 160°C. Remove the salmon to serve and scoop any excess sauce onto the top of the filets for extra gooey flavour. Enjoy.

STICKY BEEF & BROCCOLI

INGREDIENTS

- 1 Red onion
- 3 Garlic cloves
- 1 Broccoli head
- 700g of Steak
- 3 tablespoons of Sesame oil
- 1 tablespoon of Cornflour
- 2 tablespoons of Olive oil
- 4 tablespoons of Brown sugar
- 1 Beef stock cube of beef OXO cube
- 4-5 tablespoons of Soy sauce

Serves	4
Difficulty	●○○
Functions	Sear/Sauté
Time Prep	3-4
Time Cook	13

METHOD

1. Wash and chop the broccoli into mouth sized florets. Peel and dice the onion and the garlic cloves. Slice the steak in thin strips. Remove accessories from the cooking pot and add olive oil and sesame oil. Select SEAR/SAUTÉ on the high setting. Add the meat and brown for 2 minutes. Add the onion and garlic and sauté further until onions caramelise. Add 150ml of water, soy sauce and beef stock. Stir in the sugar.

2. Fit the pressure lid, switch the vent dial to SEAL, select PRESSURE and pressure cook on the high setting for 10 minutes. Let it release naturally after cooking. Add the broccoli. Select SEAR/SAUTE and use the medium-high setting. The broccoli should cook from the heat of the surrounding meat. If you don't like your broccoli crunchy, maybe microwave it or steam it first. Mix 2 tablespoons of water with cornflour and add it to the pot. Stir well for 3 minutes and serve with rice or egg noodles.

TOAD IN THE HOLE & GRAVY

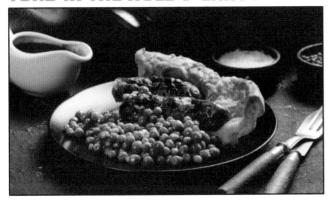

INGREDIENTS FOR TOAD IN THE HOLE

- 4 British/Irish pork sausages
- 2 medium-sized Eggs
- 120g of Plain flour
- 120ml of Whole milk
- 2 tablespoons of butter or 3 tablespoons of sunflower oil
- Salt & Pepper

Serves	2-4
Difficulty	●○○
Functions	**Bake/Roast** **Air crisp**
Time Prep	**5+**
Time Cook	**40**

INGREDIENTS FOR ONION GRAVY

- 2 Onions
- 1 dessert spoon of olive oil
- ½ a teaspoon of Mustard
- 500ml of boiling Water
- 1 Beef stock cube or 1 beef OXO cube
- Cornflour to thicken the gravy (optional)

METHOD

1. You will need a cake tin for this recipe, ideally one that fits into the Foodi on top of the steaming rack when the horizontal shelf of the rack is closest to the bottom of the cooking pot.

2. Boil a kettle. Remove the sausages from the refrigerator and allow to warm up to room temperatures.

3. Take a large mixing bowl and add the flour. Crack the eggs and use a whisk to combine the eggs to the flour. Carefully add the milk bit-by-bit while whisking to ensure no lumps are in the mixture. Add a few pinches of salt and pepper. Place the mixture into the refrigerator to chill.

4. Put the air crisp basket into the Foodi and add the sausages to it. Select AIR CRISP and cook at 180°C for 12 minutes, checking and turning often if they start to burn.

5. For the onion gravy, heat a heavy-based frying pan over a low heat. Peel and dice the onions. Add the oil, onions and a pinch of salt. Cook gently for 15–20 minutes, or until completely collapsed and dark golden-brown in colour. If the onions are cooking too quickly, then cover with a lid while they cook.

6. Remove the air crisp basket from the Foodi and put them on a plat until later. Remove the crisping basket and put the steaming rack into the cooking pot with the horizontal platform closest to the bottom of the pot. Place the cake tin on top of the rack.

7. Add the butter or sunflower oil to the cake tin and select BAKE/ROAST. Cook for 7 minutes at 210°C. This is to ensure that the butter or oil is piping hot.

8. Once the onions are completely softened and a dark golden-brown colour, stir in the mustard and add a pinch of pepper and then add the boiling water and the stock

cube. Bring the mixture to the boil, reduce to a simmer and simmer for 10–15 minutes, or until the volume of liquid has reduced by half. Taste and adjust the seasoning as necessary.

9. Remove the mixing bowl from the refrigerator. Carefully place the cooked sausages into the butter or oil and pour the contents of the mixing bowl over the sausages and use a silicone spatula to ensure that all of the mix has been scraped out of the bowl.

10. Close the lid and select AIR CRISP. Cook for 20 minutes at 210°C. During the first 15 minutes, make sure you do not open the lid otherwise the mixture that has risen will sink again.

11. Open the lid, remove the cake tin and serve with a plastic spoon or fish slice. Serve with your favourite vegetables and plenty of gravy. Enjoy.

AIR CRISPED PORK LOIN

INGREDIENTS

- Pork loin, whole
- Olive oil
- Salt & Pepper

Serves	2-5
Difficulty	●●○
Functions	Air crisp
Time Prep	1
Time Cook	22

METHOD

1. Put the steaming rack into the cooking pot, on the lowest orientation and put 1 or 2 well-oiled and well-seasoned pork loins on it.

2. Select AIR CRISP and cook at 190°C for 22 minutes.

TOMATO PASTA BAKE WITH CHICKEN & GARLIC

INGREDIENTS

- 1 Onion
- 2 Garlic cloves
- ¼ of a teaspoon of Chili flakes
- 2 x 400g cans of chopped Tomatoes
- 1 teaspoon of Sugar
- 6 tablespoons of Mascarpone
- 4 skinless chicken breasts
- 300g of penne dried pasta
- 70g of mature Cheddar cheese
- 50g of Mozzarella cheese
- ½ a small bunch of fresh Parsley
- 4 tablespoons of Olive oil
- Salt & Pepper to season

Serves	5-6
Difficulty	●●○
Functions	Sear/Sauté Bake/Roast
Time Prep	7
Time Cook	40

METHOD

1. Boil a kettle. Peel and dice the onion into very small cubes. Peel the garlic cloves. Remove the leaves from the parsley and chop them finely.

2. Take a small bowl and grate the mozzarella cheese into it. Grate the Cheddar cheese into the same bowl. Add the chopped parsley to the cheese and mix well with a fork.

3. Take the chicken breasts and slice them into mouth-sized strips.

4. Take a large saucepan and put plenty of boiling water into it, salt well. Add the penne pasta and follow the cooking instructions so that you know how long it takes to cook. Continue with the recipe but do not forget about the pasta. When it is cooked, drain the water with the aid of a sieve or a colander and prop on top of the empty saucepan until needed.

5. Open the Foodi lid and remove accessories.

6. Add a tablespoon of olive oil into the cooking pot. Select SEAR/SAUTE using the high setting. When the oil is hot, add the chicken breast and season with salt and pepper. Allow the chicken to sear for 5 minutes, stirring to avoid burning or sticking. When the chicken is cooked, remove from the pot with the aid of a large plastic spoon or simply empty the pot into a bowl using oven gloves.

7. Add 2 tablespoons of olive oil into the cooking pot and select SEAR/SAUTE using the medium setting. When the oil is hot, add the chopped onion and stir in the oil for a minute. Crush the garlic cloves one-by-one into the pot and stir-in. Add the chili flakes and cook for a further minute. Add the chopped tomatoes and the sugar. Season with some salt and pepper.

8. Switch the temperature setting down to low and allow the mixture to simmer, occasionally stirring, for 15 minutes.

9. Stir in the mascarpone cheese as soon as the sauce has thickened.

10. Empty the drained pasta back into the saucepan and add the remaining tablespoon of olive oil. Toss the pasta well in the oil using spoons until all is oiled.

11. Add the chicken back into the pot, on top of the sauce and throw in the pasta. Mix the contents really well using a wooden spoon. Press STOP on the front of the Foodi. When the pasta and sauce is mixed well, cover it completely with the contents of the small bowl, the cheeses and the parsley. Sprinkle it all over. Close the Foodi lid.

12. Select BAKE/ROAST and bake the contents at 190°C for 15 minutes. Check in the last few minutes that nothing is burning. Use a fork to test if the top layer has firmed-up. If not, add a few more minutes to the BAKE/ROAST time by pressing the time increase button.

13. Use a fish slice to serve and plate it up with some fresh salad on the side. Enjoy.

THICK PORK SAUSAGES

INGREDIENTS

■ Thick pork sausages

METHOD

Serves	1-3
Difficulty	●○○
Functions	**Air crisp**
Time Prep	**0**
Time Cook	**18**

1. Pre-heat the Foodi for 3 minutes using the BAKE/ROAST function.

2. Add 2-6 thick pork sausages to the air crisp basket and place the basket in the Foodi. Select AIR CRISP and cook at 180°C for 15 minutes. Check regularly and turn half way through.

WINTER WARMING IRISH BEEF STEW

INGREDIENTS

- 1kg of Stewing Steak or Goulash beef
- 2 tablespoons of Butter
- 1 large Onion
- 2 stalks of Celery,
- 2 tablespoons of Tomato puree concentrate

Serves	4-6
Difficulty	●●○
Functions	**Pressure Sear/Sauté**
Time Prep	5
Time Cook	75

- 1 teaspoon of dried Thyme or a sprig or two of fresh Thyme leaves
- 3 large Carrots
- 500g of potatoes
- 1/2 a can of Guinness or any other stout beer
- 350ml of boiling water
- 2 Beef stock cubes or 2 beef OXO cubes
- 2 teaspoons of Cornflour
- 1/2 a handful of fresh Parsley
- 1 teaspoon of Salt
- 1/2 teaspoon of ground Black pepper
- Olive oil

METHOD

1. Peel and dice the onion. Chop the celery into thin half-moons. Peel and chop the carrots into large chunks. Peel (if you want to) and chop the potatoes into large (larger than mouth-sized) chunks.

2. Pluck fresh parsley from the stalks and chop roughly.

3. Remove thyme from the stalks if using fresh thyme. Boil a kettle.

4. Chop the beef into large 2 cm cubes and dry using kitchen paper if you have some. Spread the meat out onto a plate and season well with salt and pepper.

5. Open the Foodi lid, remove any accessories and add a tablespoon of olive oil into the cooking pot. Select SEAR/SAUTÉ using the high setting.

6. When the oil is hot, add the beef to the cooking pot, searing it well and stirring from time to time so that nothing sticks to the base. Every chunk should be browned where possible and this can take between 4 to 5 minutes. Remove the beef and sit it on a plate for later

7. Add a further splash of oil and throw in the onion. Then add the celery shortly after.

8. When the onion has become glassy or caramelised, add the tomato puree concentrate and stir very well. If the tomato starts to spit, you can reduce the heat from the high setting to a medium setting. Cook for a further minute

9. Add half a can of Guinness or similar stout, stirring well and letting it boil for a few minutes. With the aid of a wooden spoon or silicone spatula, rub the inside of the cooking pot to remove any parts of burnt meat or onion that could be stuck there, releasing its flavour.

10. Add the thyme, 350ml of boiling water, the beef stock cube and carefully add the beef back into the pot.

11. Install the pressure lid and switch the vent dial to SEAL. Select PRESSURE and cook for 30 minutes on high. This will soften up the meat. A long time will be required to get up to the high pressure due to the amount of liquid in the pot.

12. When the pressure cooking has finished and the countdown timer has reached zero, allow the counter to count up to 10 minutes in order to naturally release pressure, aiding the meat to hold together.

13. After the 10 minutes has elapsed, switch the vent dial to VENT to quick release any further pressure. Remove the lid. We will need the lid again soon, so do not clean it or put it away.

14. Add the potatoes and carrots, stirring so all are mixed up. Apply the pressure lid again, switching the vent dial to SEAL. Select PRESSURE and cook using the high setting for 3 minutes. Again, the longest time will be reaching cooking pressure, so do not be alarmed if this takes up to 10 minutes to do.

15. In a measuring jug, add the cornflour then pour some water from the kettle to produce a thick paste, mix it so that there are no lumps. We will use this to thicken the sauce.

16. After the countdown timer has reached zero, switch the vent dial to VENT to allow a quick release of pressure. Remove the pressure lid.

17. Stir in the cornflour mix and use the KEEP WARM button on the Foodi to allow the sauce to thicken.

18. When the desired thickness of the sauce has been reached, dish out into bowls or deep plates, garnishing with chopped parsley. Enjoy

COCKTAIL SAUSAGES, POTATOES & GREEN BEANS

INGREDIENTS

- 400g potatoes
- 400g cocktail sausages, mini hotdogs or chicken nuggets
- 300g frozen green beans
- Sunflower oil
- Salt and pepper

Serves	3-4
Difficulty	●○○
Functions	**Air crisp**
Time Prep	**3**
Time Cook	**25**

METHOD

1. Wash and scrub the potatoes

2. Cut the potatoes into mouth-sized pieces, add into a deep bowl.

3. Add one dessert spoon full of sunflower oil, a few pinches of salt, a pinch of pepper and toss the potatoes so that they are completely coated with a light covering of oil.

4. Add the air crisp basket to the cooking pot and tip the potatoes into it.

5. Use the same bowl from step 3 and add the cocktail sausages to it, as well as the green beans. The beans do not need to be defrosted. Add half a dessert spoon of oil to the bowl and again toss the contents until all items are covered in oil.

6. Tip the contents on top of the potatoes. Any excess oil will drip through the base of the air crisp basket so do not worry if you think too much oil has been used.

7. Close the lid and select AIR CRISP. Cook at 180°C for 25 minutes. Half-way through the cooking time, open the lid and with a wooden spoon or a silicone spatula, stir the contents around so that the potatoes from the bottom of the pot are now at the top of the pot.

8. Remove from the Foodi and enjoy!

TIPS

If you would prefer, replace the sunflower oil with a knob of melted butter. This will provide a much more satisfying taste!

The sausages can be replaced by chicken nuggets. Timing remains the same if the nuggets are frozen.

LANCASHIRE VEGGIE HOTPOT ⓥ

This recipe boasts all of your five-a-day in a single serving. Shed-loads of vegetables cooked under a layer of creamy, yet crispy potatoes, all topped with cheese!

INGREDIENTS

- 500g of Potatoes
- 1 Red onion
- 2 Garlic cloves
- 1 Carrot
- 1 Leek
- 100g of fresh or frozen Broccoli florets
- 100g of fresh or frozen Cauliflower florets
- 2 small Turnips or half a Swede.

Serves	4
Difficulty	●●○
Functions	**Pressure Sear/Sauté Bake/Roast**
Time Prep	**10**
Time Cook	**45**

- 1 tablespoon of Plain flour
- 2 tablespoons of Olive oil
- 700ml of boiling Water
- 1 – 2 Vegetable stock cubes or vegetable OXO cubes
- Salt & Pepper to season
- 150ml of Dry cider (such as Strongbow or supermarket equivalent)
- 1 Apple
- 2 tablespoons of fresh or 1 tablespoon of ground Sage
- A pinch or two of ground Cayenne pepper
- 50g of (grated) Cheddar cheese

METHOD

1. Boil a kettle with 1 litre of water in it. Peel the potatoes and slice into thin ½ cm slices. Place the potatoes into the cooking pot. Add 200ml of water. Fit the pressure cooker lid, turn the vent dial to SEAL. Select PRESSURE and cook on HIGH for 5 minutes. Quick release (switch the vent to the VENT position).

2. Remove the potatoes from the Foodi, draining any residue water using a colander or a sieve and keep the potatoes for later in the recipe.

3. Peel and halve the red onion. Slice into thin slices. Peel the garlic cloves. Chop the bottom ½ a centimetre off the leek and slice into 1cm thick rings. Peel the carrot and chop into 2cm cubes/chunks. Cut the turnip into quarters or the swede into mouth-sized chunks.

4. Take a measuring jug and add 700ml of boiling water. Add the stock cubes and dissolve them.

5. Peel, core and slice the apple. If the Cheddar cheese is not grated, grate it into a small bowl for later.

6. Add 2 tablespoons of olive oil to the cooking pot and select SEAR/SAUTE using the high setting. When the oil is hot, add the onion and the leek. Crush the garlic into the pot and stir occasionally, cooking for 2 to 3 minutes. Add the broccoli, the cauliflower, the turnip or swede, the carrot, stirring well for a further 4 minutes.

7. Stir in the flour and cook for 1 minute. Slowly introduce the measuring jug of stock to the pot, slowly stirring the ingredients. Do the same with the cider.

8. Allow the contents to come to the boil. Add the chopped apple, the sage and the cayenne pepper and season with some salt and pepper. If you used 2 stock cubes, the pot may be salty enough, so be careful. Mix well.

9. Turn off the Foodi. Slowly and carefully add the potato slices to the top of the pot, overlapping each other so as to create a roof on the vegetables.

10. When the complete top of the pot is covered in potato, sprinkle grated Cheddar cheese across the potato.

11. You may also add some dried chives for decoration if you so wish.

12. Close the built-in lid and select BAKE/ROAST. Cook at 180°C for 25 minutes. During the last 5 minutes, check that the hotpot is not burning and make sure the potato is golden brown, crisping at the edges.

13. When the time is up and the hotpot is cooked, use a silicone spatula to free the edges of the hotpot from the cooking pot, serve with a plastic spoon or ladle and enjoy.

CHEESE & CHIVE SCONES ⓥ

INGREDIENTS

- 225g of self-raising flour
- ½ a teaspoon of salt
- ½ a handful of fresh Chives
- 100ml of Skimmed or Semi-skimmed Milk
- 60g of Mature cheddar cheese
- 100g of low-fat Soft cheese (such as Philadelphia, ideally the version with added herbs). Keep a little extra to spread inside the finished scones.
- 1 tablespoon of Powdered mustard
- ½ a teaspoon of Cayenne pepper

Serves	8 scones
Difficulty	●●○
Functions	**Bake/roast**
Time Prep	**10**
Time Cook	**17**

METHOD

1. Chop the fresh chives into roughly 2mm long tubes. Grate the Cheddar cheese into a bowl. Sift the flour with the aid of a sieve into a mixing bowl.

2. Also add the mustard powder, cayenne pepper and the salt. Add the soft cheese and the chives, mix both well into the mix with a silicone spatula.

3. Create a well in the centre of the mixture and slowly, bit-by-bit add the 100ml of milk, stirring all the time until a soft dough has been formed.

4. Shake some flour out onto your work surface and turn out the dough. Knead it gently. With the aid of a floured-rolling pin, roll out the dough until it is about 2cm thick.

5. Use a 5 cm (or thereabouts) biscuit cutter, which has been dipped in flour, to cut out as many scones as possible from the dough.

6. Knead the dough together again, roll out and cut out until all the dough has been used. I find that this recipe yields around 10 scones. Brush the tops of each scone with milk and sprinkle with grated Cheddar cheese.

7. Open the lid of the Foodi and place the air crisp basket into the cooking pot. Select BAKE/ROAST and cook at 170°C for 2 minutes to pre-heat the device.

8. Grease the basket lightly with margarine or butter. Fit as many of the scones that will fit into the basket and close the lid.

9. Select BAKE/ROAST and cook for 11 minutes at 180°C, checking in the last few minutes that they are not too brown. If they are not quite ready, add a few more minutes to the timer using the temperature up button.

10. Remove from the air crisp basket and allow to cool a little on a wire rack. Repeat from stage 5 for the rest of the scones. Slice a scone in half and spread with soft cheese. Serve warm and enjoy

HALLOUMI WITH COURGETTE & POTATO CASSEROLE ⓥ

INGREDIENTS

- 2 Leeks
- 2 Courgettes
- Olive oil
- 300g of Crème fraiche
- 4 teaspoons Paprika
- 1kg of new or baby Potatoes
- 400g of Halloumi cheese
- 4 teaspoons of Vegetable stock powder or vegetable stock cubes
- A handful of fresh Parsley
- Half a handful of fresh Chives
- 4 teaspoons of Cornflour
- Salt & Pepper to season

Serves	4
Difficulty	●●○
Functions	Pressure Sear/Sauté
Time Prep	5
Time Cook	25

METHOD

1. Boil a kettle with at least 1 litre of water in it. Wash the potatoes and cut them into mouth-sized chunks. Wash the courgettes and remove the ends. Cut them lengthways, rotate, then cut again lengthways, chop into small quarter circle rounds, ½ cm thick. Pluck the parsley and chop the leaves finely. Chop the chives into 3mm long tubes. Chop the roots off the end of the leeks, slice lengthways and pull apart the pieces to wash them thoroughly. Stack them back together and slice into 1cm wide strips. Dry the halloumi cheese with kitchen paper and slice into roughly 2cm cubes

2. Pour 1 litre of boiling water into a measuring jug. Add the vegetable stock and stir it to dissolve the stock.

3. Remove the air crisp basket from the cooking pot and pour in the jug of stock. Add the potatoes. Install the pressure lid and switch the vent dial to SEAL. Select PRESSURE and cook on the high setting for 3 minutes. When the countdown timer has reached zero, switch the vent dial to VENT and release the pressure quickly.

4. During the pressure-cooking time above, heat a frying pan on the stove (highest heat setting) and add a dessert spoon of olive oil. When the oil is hot, carefully add the halloumi cubes and monitor them as they brown. Turn as soon as they brown so that at least two sides of each cube is crispy-brown. Remove them from the pan and keep for later.

5. Take a small bowl and add the cornflour. Add a few spoonful's of water and mix quickly to form a paste. Remove the pressure lid and add the cornflour paste. Mix well to thicken the liquid in the pot using a wooden spoon or silicone spatula Select SEAR/SAUTE using the high temperature setting. Cook the pot contents for 2 minutes.

6. Add the leek and courgette and mix them in well, ensuring that they are underneath the potato chunks. Fit the pressure lid again and make sure the vent dial is switched to VENT. Allow the contents to continue to cook for 4 minutes. Remove the lid, add the crème fraiche, the paprika and some salt and pepper to taste. Stir in the parsley.

7. Dish out into four deep plates. Add halloumi cubes to the top of each and sprinkle with fresh chives. Crack a little pepper over the top. Enjoy

ONE POT GLAZED CHICKEN THIGHS WITH BUTTERNUT SQUASH MASH

INGREDIENTS

- 2 fresh Chicken thighs
- ½ a Butternut squash
- 3 tablespoons of Whole milk
- Dried mixed herbs
- Sea salt and Black pepper
- A small bunch of fresh chives
- Barbecue sauce
- Sesame seeds to garnish

Serves	2
Difficulty	●●○
Functions	Pressure Sear/Sauté Air crisp
Time Prep	5
Time Cook	25

METHOD

1. Remove all accessories from the cooking pot.

2. Roughly chop the butternut squash into 1-2cm cubes and place the cubes into the cooking pot. Add 400ml of water, a pinch of salt and place the steaming rack above the squash with the horizontal part of the rack closest to the bottom of the pot. Chop the chives into 2mm long tubes. Keep the chives for decoration.

3. Dry-rub the chicken thighs with sea salt. Add cracked black pepper onto the chicken. Sprinkle dried mixed herbs onto the chicken (supermarket mixed herbs are usually: Thyme (40%), Marjoram (19%), Oregano, Parsley, Sage, Basil).

4. Sit the thighs on top of the steaming rack. Fit the pressure lid. Switch the vent dial to SEAL and pressure cook on the high setting for 11 minutes. Switch the vent dial to VENT to quick release the pressure.

5. Remove the chicken and the rack and place on a plate to catch any drips. Drain off any excess water from the pot and add the milk.

6. Select SEAR/SAUTÉ on the medium setting. Use a silicone spatula or plastic spoon to mash the squash, avoiding scratching the pot.

7. Add salt and pepper to taste and a sprinkle of the mixed herbs.

8. Put the steaming rack together with the chicken back on top of the mash.

9. Coat the chicken with barbecue sauce using a pastry brush. Don't be scared, if it is a thick sauce, add plenty.

10. Select AIR CRISP and cook for 8 minutes at 200°C.

11. Mix the mash with any oil and juices that have dripped from the chicken using the spatula.

12. Serve onto 2 plates in the centre, coat with a sprinkle of chives and sit the chicken thigh on top. Any remaining chives can be sprinkled onto the plates. Enjoy.

HOT & SPICY CHICKEN DOPIAZA

INGREDIENTS

- 5 Red onions
- 5 Garlic cloves
- A thumb-sized piece of Ginger
- 3 Green chilis
- 4 tablespoons of Olive, groundnut or rapeseed oil

Serves	6-8
Difficulty	●●○
Functions	**Sear/Sauté**
Time Prep	**15**
Time Cook	**45**

- 10-12 Chicken breast fillets, depending on size
- 1 teaspoon of Honey
- 3 teaspoons of ground Cumin
- 1 teaspoon of ground Turmeric
- ¼ to ½ a teaspoon of ground Red chili (Cayenne if you like it spicy)
- ½ a teaspoon of ground black Pepper
- 1 teaspoon of Aniseeds
- 2 Chicken stock cubes or 2 chicken OXO cubes
- 750ml of boiling Water
- ½ teaspoon of Saffron strands (optional)
- 120ml of Whole milk
- 250ml of Natural yoghurt
- 3 tablespoons of Sour cream
- Rice to serve (see the Side dish recipes)
- ¼ teaspoon of salt

METHOD

1. Boil a kettle with 800ml of water in it.

2. Pour the milk into a small bowl and add the saffron to it. Peel and chop the onions into mouth-sized chunks. Peel the garlic. Peel the ginger. Slice the chilis lengthways and remove the seeds.

3. Put half of the onions, all of the chilis, the ginger and all of the garlic into a large measuring jug. Use a hand blender to blend the mixture together into an aromatic paste.

4. Chop the chicken into slightly larger than mouth-sized pieces. Open the Foodi lid and add 1 tablespoon of the oil into the cooking pot.

5. Select SEAR/SAUTE using the high temperature setting.

6. When the oil is hot, add the chicken and stir around for about 4 to 5 minutes, until all the chicken is browned on all sides. When the chicken is brown, carefully empty the cooking pot of its contents into a large bowl. Return the cooking pot to the Foodi.

7. Add the remainder of the oil and add the rest of the onion chunks and stir them until they have softened. Don't go overboard with the stirring, as the onions are better when kept in large chunks, rather than fallen apart.

8. Add the cumin, turmeric, pepper, salt, ground chili and aniseeds and stir well for 3 to 4 minutes, until aromatic.

9. Add the garlic and onion paste mix to the pot and the honey. Keep stirring, so that it does not stick to the base, for 5 minutes.

10. Add 750ml of boiling water, the chicken breast and crumble in the stock cubes.

11. Reduce the temperature to the medium setting and let it cook for 15 minutes. In the measuring jug from earlier, add the yoghurt and the sour cream and mix it well.

12. When the 15 minutes is up, mix the saffron milk with the yoghurt-cream in the measuring jug and slowly add that mixture to the curry.

13. Apply a lid (glass if you have one, otherwise the pressure lid with the vent dial switched to VENT) and continue to cook for a further 15 minutes on the low-medium temperature setting.

14. When the sauce has thickened, serve with rice and enjoy.

CHEATERS SCOTCH EGGS

INGREDIENTS

- 1 pack of 8 Pork sausages
- 5 Eggs
- Breadcrumbs
- Olive oil

Serves	4
Difficulty	●●○
Functions	Sear/Sauté Air crisp
Time Prep	10
Time Cook	25

METHOD

1. Boil 4 of the eggs in a pan of boiling water for 6 minutes. Cool the eggs under cold water. Peel the shell from the eggs. De-case all 8 sausages, 2 sausages will be used per egg. Crack the final egg into a bowl and beat it. Pour breadcrumbs into a large bowl

2. Take the meat of two sausages and wrap it around an egg. Dip it in beaten egg, then coat it in breadcrumbs. Repeat for all eggs.

3. Pre-heat the foodi for 4 minutes by selecting BAKE/ROAST at 190°C. Spray the air crisp basket with oil. Add the scotch eggs to the air crisp basket, place it in the cooking pot and select AIR CRISP. Cook for 16 minutes at 190°C. Turn regularly and serve when finished.

CRISPY TURKEY STEAKS

INGREDIENTS

- 4 or 5 fresh Turkey "minute steaks"
- 180g of Plain flour
- A large bag or 2 small bags of Bacon flavoured crisps
- 2 Eggs
- Salt & Pepper to season

Serves	4-5
Difficulty	●●○
Functions	**Air crisp**
Time Prep	15
Time Cook	10

METHOD

1. With the aid of a meat hammer (or use a sheet of greaseproof paper, folded over the meat and use your fists), beat the turkey steak into very thin slices, ideally 1cm thick or less.

2. Season both sides of the meat with salt and pepper.

3. Arrange 3 deep plates on the worktop. Open the bag(s) of crisps and flatten with the aid of a rolling pin. The crisp crumbs go in one plate/bowl.

4. Crack the eggs into the second plate/bowl and mix them up with a fork.

5. Add the flour into the final plate/bowl and add half a teaspoon salt. Mix well.

6. Take each turkey minute steak and first roll them in flour, then in egg and finally in the crisps.

7. Repeat until all parts of all steaks are coated.

8. If you have time, or if you have read ahead, place the final plate/bowl of crisp-coated steaks into the refrigerator for half an hour to keep cool and let them firm up.

9. Remove from the refrigerator and spray them lightly with oil. Add the air crisp basket to the cooking pot and carefully add the steaks to it. Do not stack the steaks unless you have a mesh or two-layered steaming rack, in which case, regularly alternate to prevent burning.

10. Select AIR CRISP.

11. Cook on air crisp for 10 minutes at 200°C. Serve with mashed potato and rocket salad, for example. Enjoy.

TIP

You can also use cornflakes in place of the bacon flavoured crisps if you so wish. Personally, I find turkey screams out for extra flavour, so bacon crisps is my recommendation.

I've also tried cheese and onion flavoured crisps in place of the bacon crisps. During the seasoning of the turkey stage, use ground sage instead of pepper to give an almost stuffing-like edge to the steak.

CHINESE-STYLE ORANGE CHICKEN

INGREDIENTS

- 500g of boneless, skinless Chicken breast fillets
- 2 large or 3 small Garlic cloves
- Roughly 2 tablespoons of Olive oil
- 175ml of Orange juice
- 4 tablespoons of Soy sauce
- 4 tablespoons of Brown sugar
- 4 tablespoons of Cornflour
- Zest of an orange to garnish (optional)
- Pepper to season (do not add salt, the soy sauce has you covered regarding salt)
- Rice to serve with
- Sesame seeds to garnish (optional)

Serves	4
Difficulty	●○○
Functions	Sear/sauté Pressure
Time Prep	5
Time Cook	25

METHOD

1. Start to cook rice as this recipe only takes about 25 minutes in total to complete. Cut the chicken breast fillets into mouth-sized cubes. Peel the garlic cloves and press/crush them into a small bowl.

2. Measure about 50 to 60ml of cold water into a cup and add the cornflour. Mix it well into a thick paste that contains no powder using a fork. Keep this bowl of cornflour paste close to the Foodi for immediate usage after pressure cooking has finished.

3. Remove all accessories from the cooking pot and add the 2 tablespoons of olive oil. Select SEAR/SAUTE using the high setting. When the oil is hot, add the chicken breast, the garlic and stir in well. Keep stirring until all of the chicken is browned, roughly 5 to 6 minutes. Switch off the Foodi. Add the orange juice, the soy sauce and the brown sugar, stirring in really well so that the sugar does not stick to the pot. Season with pepper and stir in.

4. Fit the pressure lid and switch the vent dial to SEAL. Select PRESSURE and pressure-cook using the high setting for 5 minutes. When the countdown timer has reached zero, it will begin to count up as it releases pressure. At 2 minutes on that counter, switch the vent dial to VENT to quick release the rest of the pressure.

5. When the lid is able to be easily removed, immediately take it off and scoop in the cornflour paste. Immediately stir it through the chicken with a wooden spoon or silicone spatula. This step has to be performed quickly.

6. Let the chicken sit in the base of the cooking pot for 5 minutes as the cornflour thickens into a coating on the chicken. Serve with rice (egg-fried-rice is even better served with Chinese orange chicken) and decorate with a little orange zest or ultra-thinly sliced orange. Sprinkle over some sesame seeds if you have any, this adds a little crunch. Enjoy.

MUSHROOM STROGANOFF ⓥ

INGREDIENTS

- 450g of fresh Mushrooms
- 1 tablespoon of Tomato puree (paste)
- 25g of Butter
- 1 large Onion to 2 medium-sized onions
- 1 tablespoon of wholemeal Mustard
- 150g (150ml) of Crème fraiche (or low-fat Greek yoghurt for a reduced fat version)
- A few leaves of fresh Parsley for garnish
- 1 tablespoon of ground Paprika (plus more if you would like to garnish)
- Salt & pepper to season
- 500g of Pasta

Serves	4
Difficulty	●○○
Functions	**Sear/sauté**
Time Prep	**5**
Time Cook	**15**

METHOD

1. Boil a kettle with enough water to cook the pasta, 1 litre should be more than enough. Check the cooking instructions of your pasta to work out how much time the pasta needs to cook for.

2. Wash and chop the mushrooms into 5mm thick slices. If you are going to garnish with parsley, wash it under running water then pluck the leaves from the parsley.

3. Peel and dice the onion into very small cubes.

4. Remove accessories from the Foodi.

5. Pour enough boiling water into a saucepan and turn on the high heat.

6. When the water is boiling, salt the water and add the pasta to cook.

7. Select SEAR/SAUTE using the high setting.

8. Add the butter to the cooking pot and allow it to melt. When melted, lower the temperature to the medium-high setting.

9. Add the diced onion and stir well.

10. Sauté the onion for around 5 minutes, stirring occasionally and progressing when the onion is caramelised.

11. Add the mushrooms and stir them into the onion for 1 or 2 minutes until they soften.

12. Add the tomato puree and the mustard, stir in well, then <u>quickly</u> add the crème fraiche to avoid the tomato puree burning.

13. Keep stirring and allow to cook through for about 4 minutes.

14. Shake paprika powder over the top and season with salt and pepper.

15. Stir well and have a sneaky taste to see if it is salty enough.

16. When the pasta is cooked, either lower the heat until the stroganoff is ready or drain with the aid of a sieve when it is ready.

17. Dish the stroganoff out onto 4 deep plates or bowls, garnish with parsley if you wish and shake some more paprika over the top too.

18. Serve with the pasta. Enjoy

FAKE-IKEA-KÖTTBULLAR: SWEDISH MEATBALLS

- 300g of Minced beef
- 150g of button Mushrooms
- ½ a Cucumber
- 1 Carrot
- 500g of Potatoes
- 1 Onion
- 4 tablespoons of Breadcrumbs

Serves	2-3
Difficulty	●●○
Functions	**Sear/sauté** **Air crisp**
Time Prep	10
Time Cook	35

- 200ml of Double cream
- 2 tablespoons of Cranberry sauce / marmalade.
- A handful of fresh Chives
- A handful of fresh parsley
- 1 teaspoon of mild Chili pepper
- Sugar, Salt & pepper
- Olive oil
- 1 Egg
- 1 tablespoon of Milk
- A knob of Butter

METHOD

1. Boil a kettle of water. Peel the potatoes and slice them

into mouth-sized pieces.

2. When the water is boiling, add the potatoes to a large saucepan and cover them in boiling water. Add some salt and boil on a medium-high heat for between 10 and 15 minutes.

3. Wash and peel the cucumber. Chop the end off it and slice into very thin slices (maybe your cheese grater has a wide thin cucumber slicer on the side of it). Add the cucumber into a bowl. Add a little salt and sugar.

4. Peel the onion and cut it into two halves. Cut one half into thin strips and dice the other half very finely, perhaps with the aid of a food processor or chopping device.

5. Wash the mushrooms and cut them all in halves or if they are big mushrooms, into quarters.

6. Pluck the parsley and chop the leaves finely. Cut the chives into 2mm long tubes.

7. Peel the carrot and slice into 2mm thick pieces lengthways.

8. Add the carrot slices to the potatoes roughly half-way through the potato cooking time. They should not be cooked soft, rather have a little crunch to them

9. Take a large bowl and add the minced beef.

10. Add the finely diced onion, the breadcrumbs and crack the egg into it.

11. Add a tablespoon of milk, the chili pepper, salt and pepper.

12. Using the tips of your fingers, mix everything really well until a mass of meat is formed.

13. Cut the mass of meat in half and cut each half in half again.

14. From each of the four chunks of meat, form 3 equally-sized meatballs, so that you have 12 in total.

15. Place the air crisp basket into the cooking pot and select BAKE/ROAST.

16. Preheat the pot by baking for 5 minutes at 200°C.

17. When the pot has been preheated, carefully add each meatball to the air crisp basket.

18. Select AIR CRISP and cook for 5 minutes at 210°C so that each meatball browns on the outside.

19. If after the 5 minutes is up, the meatballs are not browned, use the air crisp function for a few more minutes to brown them.

20. Remove the meatballs, placing them onto a plate.

21. Empty the cooking pot of any excess oil, keeping just a little on the base of the cooking pot for the next phase.

22. Select SEAR/SAUTE using the high setting and add the strips of onion and the mushrooms. Stir regularly so that nothing sticks to the base.

23. Take a mixing bowl and add 2 tablespoons of the cream.

24. Add the rest of the cream to the cooking pot and stir in well. Season with salt and pepper.

25. When the cream is warmed through, add the meatballs back in and reduce the sear/sauté setting to medium-high.

26. If the cream starts to crisp at the edges, reduce the temperature even further to the medium setting.

27. Let the meatballs cook in the cream and vegetables for about 8 minutes, stirring from time to time so that the meatballs are rotating in the cream to cook through.

28. Take the bowl with the cucumber slices in it and tip away any juices or water that may be in it.

29. Add the contents to the mixing bowl with the cream in

it.

30. Add salt and pepper and the chopped chives.

31. Mix well to toss the cucumber salad.

32. With the aid of a sieve, drain the potatoes and carrots and return them to the saucepan.

33. Add a knob (½ a tablespoon) of butter to the saucepan and mix the potatoes and carrots so that they are coated in a little butter.

34. Add the chopped parsley and toss the contents lightly and carefully.

35. Serve the potatoes and carrots onto 2 or 3 plates.

36. Add 6 or 4 (depending on how many servings you have chosen) meatballs next to the potatoes and carrots.

37. When all meatballs have been plated-up, use a plastic ladle to drip sauce, mushrooms and onions over the meatballs, next to the potatoes.

38. Add the cucumber salad either to the side of the plates or if you would prefer not to have it mix with the sauce, use a small bowl or large ramekin for each plate.

39. At an empty part of the plate, add a tablespoon of cranberry sauce. Enjoy.

ANNOYINGLY-SIMPLE CHEESY NACHOS-TOPPER

INGREDIENTS

- 1 bag of plain Nachos
- 125g of Fresh cream cheese, such as Philadelphia
- 2 tablespoons of Sweet chili sauce
- 1 small can of Baked beans (200g can)
- Several handfuls of grated Cheddar cheese
- A handful of fresh chives to decorate

Serves	4
Difficulty	●○○
Functions	**Air crisp**
Time Prep	5
Time Cook	13

METHOD

1. Keep the bag of nachos closed until you're ready to serve. We are just going to pour them on a plate and serve with the topper.

2. Line the air crisp basket with greaseproof paper so that it covers all of the inside of the base plus at least half way up the sides. It doesn't matter how crinkled it is, we are going to serve the topper in the basket! (You can also use a Betty Crocker-style cake tin too but I find it warms through much quicker in the air crisp basket). For a slightly less appealing look but to save on the washing up, use an aluminium foil pie case.

3. Pre-heat the Foodi by selecting AIR CRISP for 5 minutes at 180°C. Chop the chives into small tubes for decoration later.

4. With the aid of a large spoon or spatula, scoop out the cream cheese into the basket onto the paper and spread it all across the base. Spoon the baked beans over the top, again so next to no cream cheese is exposed.

5. Drizzle sweet chili sauce randomly across the top and sprinkle grated cheese to cover the beans.

6. Place in the cooking pot and select AIR CRISP. Cook for 8 minutes at 180°C, checking in the last 2 minutes that the cheese is not burning.

7. Carefully remove the topper, sprinkle with fresh chives, serve in the tin or basket that it cooked in, on a tray with a biblical-amount of nachos next to it.

BREAKFAST SWIRLS

For this recipe, you will either need 4 heat-resistant ramekins or silicone muffin cases. Warning: these are so moreish and my kids adore them. Try them in a light bread roll with a dollop of brown sauce as a hangover-busting breakfast sandwich!

Serves	2-4
Difficulty	●○○
Functions	**Air crisp**
Time Prep	**5**
Time Cook	**13**

INGREDIENTS

- 8 rashers of Streaky bacon
- 4 Medium-size eggs
- A sprig of Thyme (optional)
- 1 teaspoon of Parmesan cheese (optional)
- Black pepper to season

METHOD

1. Take a ramekin or muffin case and line it around the inside edges with a rasher of bacon.

2. Repeat with another slice of bacon in the same ramekin, this time further down to the bottom and fold it so that the base of the ramekin is also lined with bacon.

3. Repeat for the other three ramekins until each has two slices of bacon in them.

4. Crack an egg into each ramekin into the centre of the bacon swirl. Season lightly with black pepper.

5. Pluck the fresh thyme and chop the leaves into very small pieces. You can quickly use an electric chopper if you have one.

6. Sprinkle the top of the eggs with a little parmesan cheese and also some of the chopped thyme leaves.

7. Place the air crisp basket into the cooking pot.

8. Select AIR CRISP and preheat for 4 minutes at 180°C for two minutes.

9. Open the lid and carefully add the four ramekins or muffin cases, being careful not to spill any of the egg.

10. Quickly close the lid and select AIR CRISP.

11. Cook for 8 minutes at 180°C. In the last minute, quickly check that the cheese topping is not burning.

12. Remove and enjoy.

LOW CALORIE COCONUTTY CHICKEN CURRY

INGREDIENTS

- 4 Garlic cloves
- 1 large Onion
- 1 Red chili (plus one more for garnish if you want it extra spicy)
- 1kg of boneless, skinless Chicken breast fillets
- 1 can / 400g of Chopped tomatoes
- 250ml of Coconut milk
- 1 tablespoon of Garam masala.
- ½ a teaspoon of Garam masala for later on.
- 1 thumb-sized chunk of Fresh ginger
- 2 tablespoons of Cornflour
- Rice to serve
- Cashew nuts to garnish
- 1 teaspoon of Olive oil
- 1 teaspoon of Sea salt
- Salt & pepper to season

Serves	4-6
Difficulty	●●○
Functions	Sear/Sauté Pressure
Time Prep	10
Time Cook	30

METHOD

1. Boil a kettle with plenty of water in it.

2. Prepare rice in a saucepan with a lid. (1 cup of rice to every 1 1/2 cups of boiling water, rinse the rice in a sieve, boil in the water. As soon as the rice has reached the boil, allow it to boil for 1 minute.

3. Reduce the heat to the lowest setting and cover with a lid. Cook slowly without removing the lid for exactly 10 minutes. Turn off the heat and leave sealed closed for a further 12 minutes.

4. Do not open the lid at any point and make sure the saucepan lid seals completely – ie, not a lid with a hole in it). As the rice is cooking, carry on with the recipe for the curry.

5. Peel the ginger and grate it into a bowl. Slice the chicken breast fillets into mouth-sized chunks. Peel and chop the onion into 1cm wide segments. Cut the end off the red chilis, slice lengthways and remove the seeds. Slice into 2mm wide strips. Peel the garlic cloves and cut into very fine slices. Open the cans of coconut milk and tomatoes.

6. Remove accessories from the cooking pot and add a teaspoon of olive oil to the pot. Select SEAR/SAUTE using the high setting.

7. When the oil is hot, add the onion. Stir regularly for about 4 minutes until the onion is caramelised but not brown.

8. Add ¾ of the ginger to the pot, keeping the rest for later. Add the garlic and the slices of one red chili, keeping the other slices to garnish later. Stir for 30 seconds.

9. Add the chicken chunks, the coconut milk, the tomatoes, a teaspoon of sea salt, a tablespoon of garam masala. Stir well with a wooden spoon, making sure nothing has stuck to the bottom of the pot.

10. Turn off the Foodi at this point and allow the contents to warm through slightly. Mix the 2 tablespoons of cornflour with 3 tablespoons of water in a small bowl. Make sure a fine paste is created and keep a spoon handy to mix it into the pot later.

11. Install the pressure lid and switch the vent dial to SEAL.

Select PRESSURE and pressure-cook on the high setting for 4 minutes. When the countdown timer has reached zero, switch the vent dial to VENT to quickly release the pressure.

12. When all of the pressure has been released, remove the pressure lid and select SEAR/SAUTE using the medium-high setting.

13. Gradually add the cornflour paste from earlier and mix it in immediately after adding each spoonful, ensuring no lumps remain.

14. Add the remaining grated ginger to the pot and add a further ½ a teaspoon of garam masala.

15. Crack a little pepper to season and if needed, a little salt. Allow the contents to thicken up nicely, stirring from time to time.

16. Dish out rice onto deep plates and serve the curry next to it. Garnish with some cashew nuts and if required, strips of red chili. Serve and enjoy.

VEGAN MASSAMAN CURRY WITH POTATOES & CHICKPEAS Ⓥ

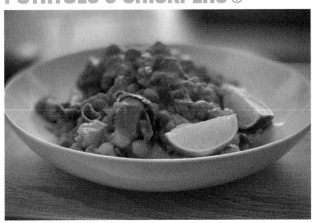

INGREDIENTS

- 1 Sweet potato
- 1 Spring onion
- 2 medium-sized Potatoes
- 1 ½ teaspoons of Vegetable stock powder or 1 vegetable stock cube
- 250ml of Coconut milk
- 1 Onion
- 1 tablespoon of Massaman curry paste
- 1 Courgette
- 1 Red chili
- 1 Lime
- 400g of Chickpeas
- 2 tablespoons of Peanut butter
- Olive oil
- Salt & pepper to season

Serves	2-3
Difficulty	●○○
Functions	Sear/sauté Bake/roast
Time Prep	10
Time Cook	45

METHOD

1. Boil a kettle with about 300ml of water in it. Preheat the Foodi by selecting BAKE/ROAST for 5 minutes at 190°C

2. Peel the potatoes and cut them into small 1cm cubes. Do the same with the sweet potato.

3. Remove the ends off the courgette, cut it lengthways through and then slice both halves into 1cm thick half-moon shapes.

4. Put all of the vegetables into a mixing bowl and add a dessert spoon full of olive oil. Toss them around to coat

them slightly. Add salt and pepper to season too.

5. Add the air crisp basket to the cooking pot.

6. Add the potatoes, the sweet potato and the courgette to the basket and select BAKE/ROAST. Cook for 18 minutes at 190°C.

7. Half way through the cooking time, remember to give them a good swish around to avoid sticking and ensure even cooking.

8. Drain the chickpeas through a sieve and run them under cold water to remove traces of the water or brine. Take a measuring jug and add 200ml of boiling water.

9. Add the vegetable stock to it and stir to dissolve.

10. Peel and cut the onion into thin strips. Cut the lime into four segments.

11. When the vegetables have finished baking, remove the air crisp basket and place it onto a heat-protected surface, such as a plate or a chopping board.

12. Add a dessert spoon of olive oil to the cooking pot. Select SEAR/SAUTE using the high setting. When the oil is hot, add the onion slices as well as the chickpeas. Stir from time to time and allow them to sauté for 4 minutes.

13. Add the curry paste and stir very well. Allow to cook for a further 2 minutes until it is smelling great. Add the prepared vegetable stock and allow it to continue to cook for 5 minutes.

14. Add the coconut milk and the peanut butter, stirring well until it thickens a little.

15. Squeeze the juice of two of the lime segments into the pot and discard the peel. Remove the ends from the spring onion and slice into thin rings.

16. Cut the chili in half lengthways and remove the seeds. Slice into 2mm thick slices.

17. Tip the vegetables from the air crisp basket into the cooking pot and mix well.

18. Allow the vegetables to warm back up for a few minutes before serving onto two deep plates.

19. Sprinkle each plate with spring onion rings, chili strips and crack some black pepper across the top, but not too much.

20. Finally add the remaining lime segments onto the side of the plate and enjoy!

MAC & CHEESE... THAT WORKS!

INGREDIENTS

- 500g of thin Macaroni pasta

- 2 Garlic cloves

- 100g of Parmesan cheese in powdered form

- 200g of grated Cheddar cheese

- 200g of grated (or thinly-sliced) Emmental cheese

- 60g (4 tablespoons) of Butter

Serves	8
Difficulty	●●○
Functions	Sear/sauté Pressure Air Crisp
Time Prep	5
Time Cook	40-45

- 30g (2 tablespoons) of Butter for the topping
- 4 tablespoons of Plain flour
- 1 teaspoon of Dijon mustard
- 2 teaspoons of ground Sweet paprika
- 2 flat teaspoons of ground Pepper
- 200ml of Whole milk
- 200ml of Cream
- 2 tablespoons of Worcestershire sauce
- 60g (8 tablespoons) of Breadcrumbs
- Salt for seasoning
- A handful of fresh Chives

METHOD

1. Peel the garlic cloves and get the garlic crusher ready for use.

2. Remove any accessories from the cooking pot and select SEAR/SAUTE using the high setting.

3. Add 30g / 2 tablespoons of butter to the pot and allow it to melt.

4. Add the breadcrumbs to it and crush the garlic cloves into the pot. Stir in really well. Allow a thick crumb to form, breaking up any large chunks with a spatula. After about 3 minutes, empty the contents of the pot into a small bowl for use later as a topping.

5. Add the 60g / 4 tablespoons of butter to the cooking pot and let it melt. Add 40g (4 tablespoons) of flour and stir it in well using a silicone spatula.

6. Add the milk, cream, paprika powder, pepper, Worcestershire sauce and the mustard. Stir well and allow to heat through. With the aid of a silicone spatula

or equivalent, empty the sauce into a bowl to keep for later. It must not be kept warm.

7. Add the macaroni to the pot and add enough water so that the macaroni is just covered.

8. Season with salt, a good shake.

9. Install the pressure lid, switch the vent dial to SEAL and select PRESSURE. Pressure-cook using the high setting for 3 minutes.

10. When the pasta has finished, let the countdown timer reach zero then count up for one minute.

11. Then, after that minute is up, switch the vent dial to VENT and quick release the rest of the pressure.

12. Using a sieve or colander, drain the cooking pot of any excess water and tip the pasta back into the pot.

13. Add the sauce back in from the bowl and add 100g of Parmesan, 200g of grated Cheddar, 200g of grated (or thinly-sliced) Emmental cheese. Using a wooden spoon or spatula, stir everything in really well until all of the cheese has melted.

14. Sprinkle by hand the topping crumbs onto the top of the mac & cheese.

15. Select AIR CRISP and cook for 20 minutes at 180°C.

16. Chop the fresh chives into 2mm long tubes.

17. Serve into deep bowls or plates, sprinkle with chives and enjoy.

18. Since this recipe serves so many people, I freeze batches of it in Tupperware.

SIDE DISH RECIPES

Of course, you may be cooking something for dinner that cannot be cooked in the Foodi, and genuinely, not everything can be! So perhaps you would like to use the Foodi to prepare the side dish, the vegetables, rice or potatoes for example.

No problem at all, the Foodi is more than capable at perfectly cooking many different types of side dishes. Some are easier to prepare than others but all of them have been tried and tested with great success.

ROAST POTATOES

GREEN BEANS WITH BACON / PANCETTA LARDONS

INGREDIENTS

- 500g of green beans (fresh or frozen)
- 1 small pack of pancetta lardons OR 3 slices of bacon
- 1 small onion or ½ a large onion
- Olive oil
- 1 vegetable stock cube
- Salt & pepper

Serves	4
Difficulty	●●○
Functions	**Sear/Sauté**
Time Prep	**3**
Time Cook	**12**

METHOD

1. Dice the onion into small cubes, placing the diced onion into the Foodi cooking pot when done.

2. Add the lardons OR dice 3 bacon slices into small pieces and add to the pot.

3. Add a glug of olive oil and select SEAR/SAUTÉ. Stir the bacon and onion with a wooden or silicone spoon until the onion is caramelised and the bacon is cooked but <u>not</u> crispy. Turn off the Foodi for a short while.

4. For fresh green beans, cup the top and tail off each bean and slice in half so that they are not too long. For frozen beans, they are usual already sold in this state. Add 500g or thereabouts to the cooking pot.

5. Add a half of a small cup or 60ml of water to the pot and a vegetable stock cube. Mix well.

6. Fit the pressure cooker lid, turn the vent to SEAL and select PRESSURE. Pressure cook for 2 minutes on the default high setting.

7. When the two minutes has ended, switch the vent to VENT and wait as the hot steam releases from the Foodi.

8. Turn off the pot and serve either as is or sprinkle with some grated cheese for extra flavour.

DID YOU KNOW?

There is a secret diagnostics menu system that allows you to check that various sensors are working correctly as well as the current status of the lids.

Simply hold down the TEMP UP and TIME UP buttons together at the same time for a few seconds to access this secret menu. Scroll through the options with the TIME UP and DOWN buttons.

Here's what I could work out from the codes as I scroll through them:

‾0:14 = Lid temperature is 14°C
_0:15 = Cooking pot temperature is 15°C
A0:P0 = Air Crisp lid open, Pressure lid not sealed
A0:P1 = Air Crisp lid open, Pressure lid sealed or Pressure lid not fitted at all
A1:P1 = Air Crisp lid closed, Pressure lid not fitted
POT1 = Cooking pot inserted correctly
POT0 = Cooking pot missing or pot sensor defect

GREEN BEANS ⓥ

INGREDIENTS

- 500g of frozen Green beans

Serves	4-6
Difficulty	●○○
Functions	**Air crisp**
Time Prep	**1**
Time Cook	**10**

METHOD

1. Add the green beans in a frozen state to the air crisp basket. Close the Foodi built-in lid

2. Select AIR CRISP. Cook for 10 minutes at 200°C. Check in the last two minutes that the beans are not burning.

PARSNIPS ⓥ

INGREDIENTS

- 3 or 4 Parsnips

Serves	3-4
Difficulty	●○○
Functions	**Air crisp**
Time Prep	**1**
Time Cook	**14**

METHOD

1. Peel and chop the parsnips, either in circular slices or lengthways into ½ cm thick batons.

2. Add the parsnips to the air crisp basket. Close the Foodi built-in lid. Select AIR CRISP. Cook for 14 minutes at 190°C. Check in the last two minutes that the parsnips are not burning.

GRILLED BEEF TOMATOES ⓥ

INGREDIENTS

- 3 or 4 Beef tomatoes, halved

Serves	3-4
Difficulty	●○○
Functions	**Pressure**
Time Prep	**1**
Time Cook	**10**

METHOD

1. Cut the tomatoes in half.

2. Add the tomatoes to the air crisp basket. Close the Foodi built-in lid

3. Select AIR CRISP. Cook for 10 minutes at 180°C. Check in the last two minutes that the tomatoes are not burning.

GRILLED CHERRY TOMATOES ⓥ

INGREDIENTS

- 500g Cherry / cocktail tomatoes

Serves	4-6
Difficulty	●○○
Functions	**Air crisp**
Time Prep	**1**
Time Cook	**7**

METHOD

1. Add the tomatoes to the air crisp basket. Close the Foodi built-in lid

2. Select AIR CRISP. Cook for 7 minutes at 180°C. Check in the last two minutes that the tomatoes are not burning.

FROZEN CROISSANT Ⓥ

INGREDIENTS

- 1- 3 frozen Croissants

Serves	1-3
Difficulty	ооо
Functions	**Air crisp**
Time Prep	0
Time Cook	15

METHOD

1. Insert the air crisp basket into the cooking pot. Select AIR CRISP and cook at 150°C for 15 minutes. Enjoy

CRUNCHY BUTTERNUT SQUASH Ⓥ

INGREDIENTS

- 1 Butternut squash (average 1kg in weight).
- ½ cup of cold water

Serves	4-6
Difficulty	●оо
Functions	**Pressure**
Time Prep	1
Time Cook	6

METHOD

1. Rinse the squash well and remove the seeds. Slice the squash into small 2cm cubes.

2. Place the air crisp basket into the cooking pot. Add the squash by placing the cubes into the basket. Add ½ a cup of water (125ml).

3. Fit the pressure cooker lid, turn the vent dial to SEAL. Select PRESSURE and cook on LOW for 2 minutes. Quick release (switch the vent to the VENT position).

MASHED BUTTERNUT SQUASH Ⓥ

INGREDIENTS

- 1 Butternut squash (average 1kg in weight).
- 150ml of cold water

Serves	4-6
Difficulty	●оо
Functions	**Pressure**
Time Prep	1
Time Cook	10

METHOD

1. Rinse the squash well and remove the seeds. Slice the squash into small 2cm cubes.

2. Place the steaming rack lower side down into the cooking pot.

3. Add the squash by placing the cubes on top of the steaming rack.

4. Add 150ml of water.

5. Fit the pressure cooker lid, turn the vent dial to SEAL

6. Select PRESSURE and cook on HIGH for 5 minutes.

7. Quick release (switch the vent to the VENT position).

DID YOU KNOW?

Before pressure cooking or slow cooking meat, put it in the cooking pot and use the SEAR/SAUTE function for a few minutes to sear the meat. Sear all sides. This aids caramelization and locks the natural flavour into the meat.

BAKED SWEET POTATO ⓥ

INGREDIENTS

- Sweet potatoes
- Olive oil
- Salt or any other optional seasoning
- Cocktail stick or wooden skewer (to check whether they are cooked)

Serves	3-4
Difficulty	●○○
Functions	**Bake/roast**
Time Prep	**1**
Time Cook	**35**

METHOD

1. Rinse the sweet potatoes under cold water and prick each of them with a fork at least twice.

2. Carefully rub olive oil all over the skin of each sweet potato. Salt the skin of each if required.

3. Using the metal rack that came with the Foodi, so that the horizontal part is closest to the base of the cooking pot, stack each potato onto it. Close the lid of the Foodi.

4. Select BAKE/ROAST and cook the potatoes at 190°C for 35 minutes. If you have chosen several differently-sized sweet potatoes, check them regularly as the countdown approaches the zero, adding more time should some larger sweet potatoes still be firm when pricked with a wooden skewer or cocktail stick.

TIPS

When cooked, cut open, salt the inside sweet potato flesh and top them with crème fraiche and chives, or simply just a knob of butter.

SWEET POTATO – STEAMED ⓥ

INGREDIENTS

- 500g or sweet potatoes.
- 500ml of boiling water

Serves	4-5
Difficulty	●○○
Functions	**Steam**
Time Prep	**2**
Time Cook	**8-14**

METHOD

1. Boil a kettle of at least half a litre of water. Peel the sweet potatoes and cut into 1cm cubes. Place crisping basket into the cooking pot. Add the cubes of the sweet potatoes by placing the them into the basket.

2. Add 500ml of water and a ¼ teaspoon of salt. Fit the pressure cooker lid, turn the vent dial to VENT. Select STEAM and cook for 8 minutes (for crunchy sweet potatoes), or 14 minutes (for much softer pieces).

ASPARAGUS – STEAMED ⓥ

INGREDIENTS

- 1 bunch of Asparagus (white or green)

Serves	2-4
Difficulty	●○○
Functions	**Steam**
Time Prep	**1**
Time Cook	**7-15**

METHOD

1. Add the Asparagus to the steaming rack. Add 500ml of water. Install the pressure lid with vent switched to VENT. Select STEAM. Cook for 15 minutes

GREEN CABBAGE – STEAMED ⓥ

INGREDIENTS

- 1 head of Cabbage.
- 500ml of boiling water

Serves	4-5
Difficulty	●○○
Functions	Steam
Time Prep	2
Time Cook	6-12

METHOD

1. Boil a kettle of at least half a litre of water.

2. Cut the cabbage head in half, remove the core and then for each half slice 1.5cm wide strips until the whole cabbage is sliced.

3. Place the crisping basket into the cooking pot.

4. Add the slices of cabbage into the basket.

5. Add 500ml of water and a ¼ teaspoon of salt.

6. Fit the pressure cooker lid, turn the vent dial to VENT

7. Select STEAM and cook for 6 minutes (for crunchy cabbage leaves), or 12 minutes (for much soggier and pungent leaves).

DID YOU KNOW?

When pressure cooking meat, do not use the quick release method as the proteins in the meat very quickly toughen, making the meat hard to eat. Always natural release the pressure when cooking meat.

CORN ON THE COB – STEAMED ⓥ

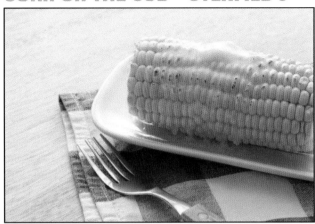

INGREDIENTS

- 4 Corn cobs
- Butter or olive oil

Serves	2-4
Difficulty	●○○
Functions	Steam
Time Prep	1
Time Cook	9

METHOD

1. Remove the husks from the corn cobs.

2. Add the corn cobs to the steaming rack. Add 475ml of water. Install the pressure lid with vent switched to VENT.

3. Select STEAM. Cook for 9 minutes, 7 minutes if only two corn cobs in the Foodi.

HASH BROWNS / RÖSTI Ⓥ

INGREDIENTS

- Hash browns, frozen

Serves	1-25
Difficulty	○○○
Functions	**Air crisp**
Time Prep	**0**
Time Cook	**12**

METHOD

1. Add the hash browns to the air crisp basket. Close the Foodi built-in lid. Select AIR CRISP. Cook for 15 minutes at 200°C. Check in the last two minutes for burning.

PEAS - STEAMED Ⓥ

INGREDIENTS

- 200g - 500g of Frozen peas

Serves	2-4
Difficulty	●○○
Functions	**Steam**
Time Prep	**1**
Time Cook	**7-15**

METHOD

1. Add the peas to the air crisp basket. Add 500ml of water. Install the pressure lid with vent switched to VENT. Select STEAM. Cook for 15 minutes

JASMINE RICE Ⓥ

INGREDIENTS

- 200g Jasmine rice
- 250ml of cold water

Serves	3-4
Difficulty	●○○
Functions	**Pressure**
Time Prep	**1**
Time Cook	**16**

METHOD

1. Rinse the rice in a sieve under cold water until the water runs clear.

2. Remove all accessories from the cooking pot. Add the rice to the cooking pot.

3. Add 250ml of water.

4. Fit the pressure cooker lid, turn the vent dial to SEAL

5. Select PRESSURE and cook on high for 4 minutes.

6. Natural release (leave the vent in the SEAL position) for 10 minutes.

7. Quick release (switch the vent to the VENT position).

WILD RICE ⓥ

INGREDIENTS

- 200g White / long-grain rice
- 600ml of cold water

Serves	3-4
Difficulty	●○○
Functions	**Pressure**
Time Prep	**1**
Time Cook	**15**

METHOD

8. Rinse the rice in a sieve under cold water until the water runs clear. Remove all accessories from the cooking pot. Add the rice to the cooking pot.

9. Add 600ml of water. Fit the pressure cooker lid, turn the vent dial to SEAL. Select PRESSURE and cook on high for 25 minutes. Natural release (leave the vent in the SEAL position) until the lid is movable.

WHITE LONG-GRAIN RICE ⓥ

INGREDIENTS

- 200g White / long-grain rice
- 300ml of cold water

Serves	3-4
Difficulty	●○○
Functions	**Pressure**
Time Prep	**1**
Time Cook	**15**

METHOD

1. Rinse the rice in a sieve under cold water until the water runs clear. Remove all accessories from the cooking pot. Add the rice to the cooking pot.

2. Add 300ml of water. Fit the pressure cooker lid, turn the vent dial to SEAL. Select PRESSURE and cook on high

for 3 minutes. Natural release (leave the vent in the SEAL position) for 10 minutes. Quick release (switch the vent to the VENT position).

LONG-GRAIN BROWN / WHOLEMEAL RICE ⓥ

INGREDIENTS

- 200g Brown / wholemeal rice
- 250ml of cold water

Serves	3-4
Difficulty	●○○
Functions	**Pressure**
Time Prep	**1**
Time Cook	**30**

METHOD

1. Remove all accessories from the cooking pot. Add 200g of brown or wholemeal rice to the cooking pot. Add 250ml of cold water. Fit the pressure cooker lid, turn the vent dial to SEAL Select PRESSURE and cook on high for 22 minutes.

2. Natural release (leave the vent in the SEAL position) for 10 minutes. Quick release (switch the vent to the VENT position).

MEDITERRANEAN POTATOES ⓥ

INGREDIENTS

- 500g of Baby potatoes
- 2 tablespoons of Tomato paste/puree
- 2 tablespoons of Olive oil
- 1 tablespoon of dried/powdered/lazy garlic
- A handful of fresh Parsley
- 2 tablespoons of Paprika
- 110g of Mayonnaise
- 2 tablespoons of white wine vinegar / brandy vinegar
- Salt & Pepper to season

Serves	3-4
Difficulty	●○○
Functions	**Air crisp**
Time Prep	**7**
Time Cook	**27**

METHOD

1. Wash the baby potatoes and chop each in half. Pluck the fresh parsley from the stems and chop the leaves roughly.

2. Take a large mixing bowl and add the potatoes, the paprika, the olive oil, the garlic powder, a good pinch of salt and pepper. Mix everything in well, making sure that the potatoes are all covered in the spice mix.

3. Add the air crisping basket to the cooking pot and tip the potatoes into it. Select AIR CRISP and cook at 180°C for 27 minutes. Toss them around a little halfway through cooking.

4. When air crisping has finished, tip them back into the mixing bowl. Add the mayonnaise and tomato paste/puree, the vinegar and the chopped parsley. Toss the potatoes in the mixture well, being careful not to damage the potatoes. Sprinkle a little rock salt on top if you have any. Serve and enjoy.

FRIED ONIONS ⓥ

INGREDIENTS

- 2-3 Large onions
- Olive oil

Serves	4-6
Difficulty	●○○
Functions	**Air crisp**
Time Prep	**1**
Time Cook	**10**

METHOD

1. Peel and chop the onions into eighths. Add them into a bowl and use a dessert spoon of olive oil to toss the onion in.

2. Put the air crisp basket into the cooking pot. Pour the onions into the air crisp basket and select AIR CRISP. Cook for 10 minutes at 200°C, giving them a little stir around after 5 minutes. Perfect to serve with hotdogs or burgers. Enjoy.

TANGY SPICED RICE ⓥ

INGREDIENTS

- 400g of Basmati rice
- 475ml of Boiling water
- 1 Onion
- 1 Vegetable stock cube
- 1 teaspoon of Garlic salt
- ½ teaspoon of ground Pepper
- 1 tablespoon of softened Butter
- 1 teaspoon of ground/dried/lazy Garlic

Serves	4
Difficulty	●○○
Functions	**Pressure**
Time Prep	3
Time Cook	14

METHOD

1. Peel and dice an onion. Tip the rice into a saucepan and half-fill it with cold water. After 5 minutes, use a sieve to remove the water. Tip the rice into the cooking pot. Add 475ml of boiling water and the stock cube. Stir until dissolved.

2. Add the garlic salt, the pepper, the butter, the ground garlic and the diced onion. Stir well.

3. Fit the pressure lid and switch the vent dial to SEAL. Pressure cook for 4 minutes using the high setting.

4. After the countdown timer has reached zero, allow the pressure to release naturally for 10 full minutes, then switch the dial to VENT. Stir well and enjoy.

BROCCOLI – PRESSURE COOKED ⓥ

INGREDIENTS

- 1 Broccoli head.
- ¼ teaspoon of Salt
- 2 tablespoons of Sliced almonds (optional)

Serves	4-5
Difficulty	●○○
Functions	**Pressure**
Time Prep	2
Time Cook	5

METHOD

1. Rinse the broccoli well and remove the large stem. Slice the broccoli into small florets. Place the steaming rack lower side down into the cooking pot. Add the broccoli by placing the florets on top of the steaming rack.

2. Add 150ml of water and ¼ teaspoon of salt. Fit the pressure cooker lid, turn the vent dial to SEAL Select PRESSURE and cook on LOW for 1 minute.

3. Quick release (switch the vent to the VENT position). In a bowl with the aid of a large plate to cover the top, shake the broccoli with the sliced almonds before serving

DID YOU KNOW?

If you use boiling water from the kettle to pressure cook, instead of cold water, the pressurize process takes much less time. The first few minutes of reaching pressure is heating the water up.

BROCCOLI – STEAMED Ⓥ

INGREDIENTS

- 1 Broccoli head.
- 500ml of boiling water
- ¼ teaspoon of Salt
- 2 tablespoons of Sliced almonds (optional)

Serves	4-5
Difficulty	●○○
Functions	**Steam**
Time Prep	2
Time Cook	**5-9**

METHOD

1. Boil at least half a litre of water in a kettle.

2. Rinse the broccoli well and remove the large stem. Slice the broccoli into large 2.5cm to 5cm florets.

3. Place the steaming rack lower side down into the cooking pot.

4. Add the broccoli by placing the florets on top of the steaming rack.

5. Add 500ml of water and a ¼ teaspoon of salt.

6. Fit the pressure cooker lid, turn the vent dial to VENT

7. Select STEAM and cook for 5 minutes (for firm crunchy broccoli), or 9 minutes (for soft broccoli).

8. In a bowl with the aid of a large plate to cover the top, shake the broccoli with the sliced almonds before serving

BRUSSELS SPROUTS – PRESSURE COOKED Ⓥ

INGREDIENTS

- 500g Brussels sprouts.

Serves	4-5
Difficulty	●○○
Functions	**Pressure**
Time Prep	2
Time Cook	5

METHOD

1. Rinse the sprouts well and cut each in half. Place the steaming rack lower side down into the cooking pot. Add the sprouts by placing them on top of the steaming rack. Add ½ a cup of water (125ml).

2. Fit the pressure cooker lid, turn the vent dial to SEAL. Select PRESSURE and cook on LOW for 1 minute (for crunchy sprouts, cook for 2 minutes for much softer sprouts).

3. Quick release (switch the vent to the VENT position).

BRUSSELS SPROUTS – STEAMED ⓥ

INGREDIENTS

- 500g Brussels sprouts.
- 500ml of boiling water
- ¼ teaspoon of Salt

Serves	4-5
Difficulty	●○○
Functions	**Steam**
Time Prep	2
Time Cook	**8-17**

METHOD

1. Boil at least half a litre of water in a kettle. Rinse the sprouts well and remove any black or loose leaves. Either keep the sprouts whole or slice them in half. Place the steaming rack lower side down into the cooking pot.

2. Add the sprouts by placing them on top of the steaming rack. Add 500ml of water and a ¼ teaspoon of salt.

3. Fit the pressure cooker lid, turn the vent dial to VENT. Select STEAM and cook for 8 minutes (for firm and very crunchy sprouts), or 17 minutes (for very soft mashed sprouts).

CARROTS – PRESSURE COOKED ⓥ

INGREDIENTS

- 500g Carrots.

Serves	4-5
Difficulty	●○○
Functions	**Pressure**
Time Prep	2
Time Cook	6

METHOD

1. Peel the carrots and slice into 1cm thick slices or 1cm wide batons.

2. Place the carrots into the cooking pot.

3. Add ½ a cup of water (125ml).

4. Fit the pressure cooker lid, turn the vent dial to SEAL

5. Select PRESSURE and cook on HIGH for 3 minutes (for soft carrots, cook for 2 minutes for crunchier carrots).

6. Quick release (switch the vent to the VENT position).

CARROTS – STEAMED Ⓥ

INGREDIENTS

- 500g Carrots.
- 500ml of boiling water
- ¼ teaspoon of Salt

Serves	4-5
Difficulty	●○○
Functions	**Steam**
Time Prep	1
Time Cook	**7-12**

METHOD

1. Boil at least half a litre of water in a kettle.

2. Peel the carrots. Slice them lengthways into ½cm wide batons.

3. Place the air crisp basket into the cooking pot.

4. Add the carrots by placing them into the basket.

5. Add 500ml of water and a ¼ teaspoon of salt.

6. Fit the pressure cooker lid, turn the vent dial to VENT

7. Select STEAM and cook for 7 minutes (for firm and very crunchy carrots), or 12 minutes (for very soft mashed carrots).

SPINACH – STEAMED Ⓥ

INGREDIENTS

- 500g or a bag of Spinach.
- 500ml of boiling water

Serves	4-5
Difficulty	●○○
Functions	**Steam**
Time Prep	1
Time Cook	**3-7**

METHOD

1. Boil at least half a litre of water in a kettle.

2. Rinse the spinach leaves well.

3. Place crisping basket into the cooking pot.

4. Add the spinach leaves by placing them into the basket.

5. Add 500ml of water and a ¼ teaspoon of salt.

6. Fit the pressure cooker lid, turn the vent dial to VENT

7. Select STEAM and cook for 3 minutes (for moist spinach), or 7 minutes (for much softer spinach leaves).

DID YOU KNOW?

You can buy wireless meat probes/thermometers that work well with the Foodi. Place the probe into the meat, put the meat in the pressure cooker and start cooking. The other end of the probe has a display so you can see within a few seconds, the temperature of the meat inside. That means, you can check the temperature of meat, if it's not quite ready, increase the cooking time on the Foodi, without having to release any of the pressure. So, you don't need to know how long to cook a large piece of meat any more, just switch on the thermometer and just watch the temperature. Stop pressure-cooking when the desired temperature has been reached.

KALE – STEAMED ⓥ

INGREDIENTS

- ▦ 500g or a bag of Kale.
- ▦ 500ml of boiling water

Serves	4-5
Difficulty	●○○
Functions	**Steam**
Time Prep	2
Time Cook	**7-10**

METHOD

1. Boil at least half a litre of water in a kettle.

2. Rinse and trim the kale leaves.

3. Place crisping basket into the cooking pot.

4. Add the kale into the basket.

5. Add 500ml of water and a ¼ teaspoon of salt.

6. Fit the pressure cooker lid, turn the vent dial to VENT

7. Select STEAM and cook for 7 minutes (for moist kale), or 10 minutes (for much softer kale leaves).

COURGETTE – STEAMED ⓥ

INGREDIENTS

- ▦ 500g of Courgettes, (3 large or 5 small courgettes).
- ▦ 500ml of boiling water

Serves	4-5
Difficulty	●○○
Functions	**Steam**
Time Prep	1
Time Cook	**3-7**

METHOD

1. Boil at least half a litre of water in a kettle.

2. Rinse the courgettes well. Remove the top and tail of each courgette. Slice them lengthways once and then slice them into 1/2cm wide half-moon shapes

3. Place the crisping basket into the cooking pot.

4. Add the courgette half-moons by placing them into the basket.

5. Add 500ml of water and a ¼ teaspoon of salt. Fit the pressure cooker lid, turn the vent dial to VENT

6. Select STEAM and cook for 3 minutes (for moist spinach), or 7 minutes (for much softer spinach leaves).

DID YOU KNOW?

You can open the protective grate in the built-in lid of your Foodi to clean it properly. Be careful, you might invalidate your warranty if the device is new. Not only that, the metal parts inside the lid are very sharp, so there is a big risk of cutting your hands. You will need a special screwdriver to open it, available from Amazon, for example. Search for a "T15 TORX screwdriver". It must have a hole in the end of the tip, some do not have that hole.

ROAST POTATOES Ⓥ

INGREDIENTS

- 500g Potatoes.
- 2 tablespoons of Olive or sunflower oil
- Salt
- 300ml Boiling water
- Small onion or onion powder *(optional, see tips)*

Serves	**4**
Difficulty	●○○
Functions	**Air crisp Pressure**
Time Prep	**2**
Time Cook	**25**

METHOD

1. Peel the potatoes and cut each into roughly 3cm cubes. Boil a kettle and add 300ml of boiling water to the cooking pot. Insert the air crisp basket and tip the potatoes into it.

2. Fit the pressure lid, switch the vent dial to SEAL and select PRESSURE. Pressure cook for 1 minute on the high setting. After the countdown timer has reached zero, switch the vent dial to VENT to quick release the pressure.

3. Remove the potatoes, tipping them into a deep bowl. Add 2 tablespoons of either olive or sunflower oil. Salt generously. Using a large plate on top of the bowl, toss the potatoes in the oil until each is coated. This action

allows for the edges of the potatoes to buckle and this will enable a crispier potato when roasted. Using a spoon will not damage the potatoes enough for crisping.

4. Empty the cooking pot of water. Return potatoes to the air crisp basket in the cooking pot and close the built-in lid.

5. Select AIR CRISP and cook at 200°C for 20 minutes. Half way through the cooking time, open the lid and carefully shake the potatoes in the air crisp basket to loosen them up.

TIPS

During the last stage, shake some dried onion powder to the potatoes to make them tastier and crunchier, five minutes before the cooking time is up.

Dice a small onion and pressure cook along with the potatoes. Include them during the oil coating phase. After air crisping, enjoy the fried onion taste with the roast potatoes. Perfect with a steak, beef roast dinner or liver.

During the oil phase, add dried rosemary and thyme generously.

If you want to guarantee creamier, crunchier outsides of the potatoes, before adding them for the air crisping phase, instead of stirring them with a spoon, put them in a saucepan, cover it with a plate. Holding the pan and plate securely, vigorously shake them around for a few seconds, causing serious damage to them. Add some rock salt, crumble an OXO cube on them and oil as in the recipe. Then air crisp as before.

BROWNED CAULIFLOWER BITES Ⓥ

INGREDIENTS

- 450g Cauliflower florets.
- Olive oil

Serves	4
Difficulty	●○○
Functions	**Air crisp**
Time Prep	1
Time Cook	12

METHOD

1. Cut the head of cauliflower into mouth-sized florets. In a bowl, add a dessert spoon of olive oil. Add the florets and with the aid of a spoon, toss the florets so that each is covered with oil.

2. Add the air crisp basket to the cooking pot, transfer the cauliflower to the basket and close the lid. Select AIR CRISP and cook at 180°C for 12 minutes.

3. Half way through cooking, open the lid, carefully remove the basket and shake the contents about. Use a wooden spoon to ensure that florets at the base of the basket are now at the top and able to get browned-off as cooking commences. In the last 2 minutes, check that the cauliflower is not burning.

MASHED POTATO ⓥ

INGREDIENTS

- 1kg Red potatoes.
- 150ml of boiling water
- Butter
- Milk

Serves	4-6
Difficulty	●○○
Functions	**Pressure**
Time Prep	2
Time Cook	10

METHOD

1. Boil a kettle. Peel the potatoes and slice into bite-sized chunks. Place the potatoes into the cooking pot. Add 150ml of boiling water.

2. Fit the pressure cooker lid, turn the vent dial to SEAL. Select PRESSURE and cook on HIGH for 5 to 6 minutes. Quick release (switch the vent to the VENT position).

3. Remove the potatoes from the Foodi, draining any residue water using a colander or a sieve. In a saucepan or large bowl, add a glug of milk and a knob of butter. Use a potato masher to mash the potatoes into a fine puree and serve.

YORKSHIRE PUDDING ⓥ

INGREDIENTS

- 50g of Plain flour
- 1 Egg
- 150ml of Whole milk
- Salt & Pepper
- 1 tablespoon of Olive oil
- **Note:** You will need silicone or metal muffin cases/tins to cook the Yorkshire puddings.

Serves	4
Difficulty	●●○
Functions	**Air crisp**
Time Prep	5
Time Cook	25

METHOD

1. Pre-heat the Foodi by selecting BAKE/ROAST and cook for 3 minutes.

2. In a bowl, measure and add the plain flour and add salt and pepper. Bit-by-bit add the cracked egg to the mix, stirring gently with a fork or whisk. Again bit-by-bit, add the whole milk, stirring until a light paste-like batter is created. Add one final splash and whisk until it starts to foam.

3. Arrange the muffin tins or silicone bakeware in the air crisp basket or on the up-turned steaming rack. Ensure they are not too close together because the puddings will expand when cooking. Add a little oil to each (1/4 of a tablespoon in each). Add the tins to the Foodi and bake for 5 minutes so that the oil is really hot.

4. Carefully add the batter to each tin so that each is not more than half full. Close the lid and select AIR CRISP. Cook for 15 minutes at 200°C. Do not open for the first 8 minutes, or they will sink!

CROQUETTE POTATOES ⓥ

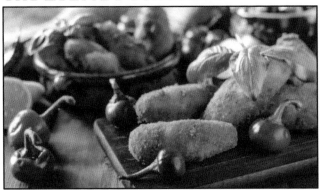

INGREDIENTS

▨ Croquette potatoes, frozen, as many as you would like

Serves	1-4
Difficulty	○○○
Functions	**Air crisp**
Time Prep	**0**
Time Cook	**16**

METHOD

1. Pre-heat the Foodi by adding the air crisp basket to the cooking pot, select BAKE/ROAST and heat for 3 minutes with the default temperature.

2. Add as many croquette potatoes as you need to the basket and do not add oil, it is not needed. Select AIR CRISP and cook for 13 minutes on 200°C, opening the lid every 2 minutes to give the basket a little shake.

TIP

Make sure you cook literally direct from frozen. If they defrost, they will lose their form or shape during cooking if they are stacked upon each other.

CRISPY BACON

INGREDIENTS

▨ 1-12 Bacon rashers

Serves	1-4
Difficulty	●○○
Functions	**Air crisp**
Time Prep	**2**
Time Cook	**10-15**

METHOD

1. Open the lid of the Foodi and place the steaming rack with the flat base closest to the top of the cooking pot.

2. Drape/hang bacon rashers over the metal slats of the steaming rack as one does with a washing line, making sure that no rashers touch the base of the cooking pot.

3. Remove the rack from the cooking pot, put some aluminium foil along the very bottom of the pot and use BAKE/ROAST to pre-heat the pot for 3 minutes.

4. Quickly add the steaming rack with bacon into the Foodi and close the lid.

5. Select AIR CRISP and cook for 10 to 12 minutes, until the bacon is as crispy as you'd like it to be. Check regularly in the last few minutes of cooking as bacon should never be wasted! Enjoy.

TIP

You can even put double slices over the steaming rack to both save space and make for less burnt or crispy bacon.

If you ruffle the aluminium foil somewhat before adding the steaming rack, you can add a few sausages on the foil and cook both at the same time. Life-changing!

ROASTED WINTER VEGETABLES Ⓥ

INGREDIENTS

- Assorted winter vegetables: such as carrots, onions, parsnips and potatoes
- Olive oil
- Dried rosemary
- Salt & Pepper

Serves	1-4
Difficulty	●○○
Functions	**Bake/Roast**
Time Prep	**2**
Time Cook	**25**

METHOD

1. Wash and peel potatoes (of leave with skin on), Cut them into mouth-sized chunks. Peel carrots and parsnips, then cut them into large chunks. Peel and chop onions into quarters. Keep the onions to one side, away from the other vegetables.

2. Load all of the chopped vegetables into a large bowl, add a dessert spoon or two of olive oil, dried rosemary, salt and pepper and toss the vegetables so that they are all oiled.

3. Add the air crisp basket to the Foodi and tip the vegetables into it. Oil the onions and keep them aside for now.

4. Select Bake/Roast and bake for 25 minutes at 180°C. Half-way through cooking, give them a good shake around and add the oiled onions.

5. If you want crunchy vegetables, select AIR CRISP and cook for 10 minutes at 180°C. Enjoy.

INDIAN-SPICED CAULIFLOWER Ⓥ

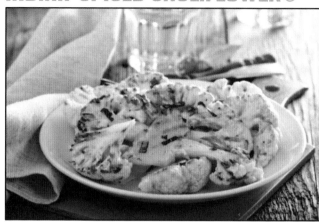

INGREDIENTS

- 1 large Cauliflower
- ½ teaspoon of Turmeric powder
- 1 teaspoon of Cumin seeds
- 1 tablespoon of dried Coriander
- 1 tablespoon of Cumin powder
- 1 teaspoon of Salt
- ½ teaspoon of Chili powder
- ½ teaspoon of Garam masala
- 1 thumb sized piece of Ginger or a teaspoon of dried ginger
- 1 Onion
- Olive oil

Serves	4-6
Difficulty	●●○
Functions	**Sear/Sauté Pressure**
Time Prep	**5**
Time Cook	**10-15**

METHOD

1. Boil a kettle with 300ml of water in it. Wash the cauliflower and cut into large florets. Peel and dice the onion. Peel and grate the ginger.

2. Remove all accessories from the cooking pot. Add a tablespoon of oil. Select SEAR/SAUTÉ using the high setting.

3. When the oil is hot, throw in the cumin seeds and stir around until they sizzle.

4. Add the diced onion and stir well until the onions are glassy and aromatic.

5. Add the turmeric, cumin powder, dried coriander, salt, chili powder, garam masala and grated ginger. Stir very well for half a minute or so.

6. Throw in the cauliflower florets and mix everything around in the pot.

7. Add 250ml of boiling water from the kettle and install the pressure lid.

8. Switch the vent dial to SEAL and select PRESSURE.

9. Pressure cook for 3 minutes using the high setting.

   When the countdown timer has reached zero, switch the vent dial to VENT.

10. Allow all the pressure to release quickly. Mix well but carefully using a wooden spoon or silicone spatula.

11. Serve and enjoy.

MUSHY PEAS Ⓥ

INGREDIENTS

- 500g of Frozen peas
- 3 sprigs of Mint
- 25g of Butter
- Salt & Pepper

Serves	4-6
Difficulty	●○○
Functions	**Pressure**
Time Prep	1
Time Cook	5

METHOD

1. Add the peas to the air crisp basket. Add 250ml of water. Install the pressure lid with vent switched to SEAL. Select PRESSURE. Cook for 1 minute, then switch the vent to VENT when finished.

2. Pour the peas into a bowl, add salt, pepper, butter and mint and mash with a potato masher or a fork. Enjoy

EXTRA-SWEET, SWEET POTATOES
Ⓥ

INGREDIENTS

- 3 medium-sized Sweet potatoes
- 2 tablespoons of Cornflour
- 4 tablespoons of Maple syrup
- 50g of Sugar
- 50g of Brown sugar
- 250ml of Water
- 2 tablespoons of Margerine

Serves	4-6
Difficulty	●●○
Functions	**Pressure**
Time Prep	**10**
Time Cook	**15**

METHOD

1. Peel the sweet potatoes and chop them into 2cm cubes. Add them into a bowl and spoon in the cornflour. Use 2 spoons to toss the sweet potato (like a salad) so that all chunks are coated.

2. Add the sweet potato chunks into the cooking pot. Add the maple syrup, the sugar, the brown sugar and also the margarine.

3. Pour over 250ml of cold water.

4. Install the pressure lid and switch the vent dial to SEAL.

5. Select PRESSURE and pressure-cook for 4 minutes using the high setting. Be aware that this much water and content will require up to 10 minutes to reach pressure before it actually starts cooking.

6. After the countdown timer has reached zero, switch the vent dial to VENT and allow for the pressure to release quickly.

7. When the pressure has fully released, you should be able to rotate and remove trhe pressure lid. Serve and enjoy.

DESSERT RECIPES

It's not just the main course where your kitchen ninja excels, wait until you see what he can whip -up for dessert!

Being such a small device compared to an oven, the Foodi lends itself well to cake baking, meaning that no part of a cake will be considerably more exposed to heat than others, in turn leading to evenly cooked on the outside, light and fluffy on the inside.

SOFT & MOIST CARROT CAKE

LEMON SPONGE CAKE Ⓥ

INGREDIENTS

- 110g of Butter, left to soften
- 200g of Caster sugar
- 2 Eggs
- 1 Lemon, washed, juiced and zested
- 190g of Plain flour
- 1 teaspoon of Baking powder
- Pinch of salt
- Cooking oil spray to grease the bundt tin
- 1 teaspoon of Vanilla extract/essence
- Icing sugar or icing to decorate

Serves	4
Difficulty	●●○
Functions	**Bake/Roast**
Time Prep	5
Time Cook	40

METHOD

1. Combine the butter, sugar and eggs in a mixing bowl, cream it all together.

2. Wash a lemon and with the aid of a cheese grater, grate the zest from the outside of the lemon.

3. Cut the lemon into two and squeeze both halves so that all the juice has been extracted

4. Carefully add the flour, baking powder, a pinch of salt, lemon juice and the vanilla extract.

5. Continue mixing until a soft dough is formed

6. Spray a bundt tin with a non-stick cooking spray (or use vegetable oil on kitchen roll to cover all parts of the inside of the tin) and spread the mix into the tin.

7. Place the tin onto the steaming rack on its lowest position, place in the Foodi and close the built-in lid

8. Set to BAKE/ROAST at 160°C for 30 minutes

9. Reduce the temperature to 140°C and bake for a further 5 minutes.

10. Carefully remove the tin from the Foodi and allow to cool for 5 minutes.

11. Release the cake from the tin and either gingerly dust with icing sugar through a sieve, or mix some icing sugar with cold water in a cup to make a water-icing. Drizzle the icing back and forth around the cake to decorate it.

BREAD AND BUTTER PUDDING ⓥ

INGREDIENTS

- 250ml of Whole milk
- 300ml of Double cream
- 1 teaspoon of Vanilla extract
- 3 Large eggs, plus 1 egg yolk from a 4th egg
- 3 tablespoons of Caster sugar
- 8 slices of Stale (but not mouldy) white crusty bread
- 50g of Butter, softened somewhat, plus some extra butter for greasing the tin
- 75g of Sultanas
- 2 - 3 tablespoons of Marmalade

Serves	4
Difficulty	●●○
Functions	**Air crisp** **Pressure**
Time Prep	5
Time Cook	85

METHOD

1. Heat the milk and cream together in a saucepan to just below the boiling point.

2. Whisk the eggs and extra egg yolk with the caster sugar in a separate bowl.

3. Pour the warm milk mixture, over the eggs, stirring constantly until smooth. Stir in the vanilla extract. This is a custard.

4. Lightly butter a cake tin.

5. Butter both sides of the bread and spread one side with marmalade

6. Cut the bread into triangles.

7. Lay half of the bread slices in the bottom of the dish so that they are slightly overlapping.

8. Sprinkle half of the sultanas over the bread.

9. Layer the rest of the bread on top then sprinkle the rest of the sultanas on.

10. Pour the custard over the bread.

11. Leave the custard to soak for at least 30 mins.

12. Place steaming rack or equivalent into the Foodi cooking pot and add 300ml of water.

13. Cover pudding tin with foil and put it on top of the rack

14. Fit the pressure lid, switching the vent dial to SEAL.

15. Select PRESSURE on the Foodi and pressure cook on high for 30 min.

16. Quick release by switching the vent dial to the VENT position

17. Remove the pressure lid.

18. Remove the tin from the Foodi, empty the water from the cooking pot, return the tin to the Foodi

19. Close the built-in lid and AIR CRISP at 180°C for 10 - 20 minutes until crisp and golden.

20. Allow to cool, don't burn yourself on that marmalade and enjoy.

Figure 7: This delicious cake recipe comes courtesy of my Mother, Hilary Small, who also loves her Ninja Foodi!

HILARY'S MARBLE BUNDT CAKE ⓥ

INGREDIENTS

- 3 Eggs
- Sugar
- Self-raising flour
- Margarine
- 1 teaspoon of Cocoa powder
- Whole milk
- 1 teaspoon of Almond essence

Serves	4-6
Difficulty	●●○
Functions	**Bake/Roast**
Time Prep	**5-10**
Time Cook	**35+**

METHOD

1. Weigh 3 eggs together including their shells using an accurate weighing scale. Keep a note of that weight. Weigh out exactly that weight of each of sugar, margarine and self-raising flour.

2. In a large mixing bowl, add the sugar and the margarine and mix/whisk it until it is fluffy.

3. Crack and add the eggs one-at-a-time while continually stirring until fully combined.

4. Add the self-raising flour gradually, folding it in with a

large spoon or spatula. Fold carefully as this makes the resulting cake light.

5. In a small bowl, add a teaspoon of cocoa powder and roughly 2 tablespoons of milk, bit-by-bit, to make into a paste.

6. Divide the cake mixture into two halves in two bowls. Add the cocoa-milk mix into one of the bowls. Add a teaspoon of almond essence to the other bowl. Fold both bowls well.

7. Grease the Bundt tin (or any cake tin that will fit into the foodi cooking pot) using margarine, dusting it with a little flour. Put alternate spoons full of the two mixtures into the Bundt tin.

8. Place the Bundt tin into the cooking pot and close the lid. Select BAKE/ROAST and cook at 180° for 14 minutes.

9. Select BAKE/ROAST again and cook this time at 160°C for 25 minutes and check it.

10. Check that it is not getting too brown/burnt. If it appears to be cooked from the outside but still gooey on the inside with the aid of a small stick, cover the Bundt tin in either a supplied Bundt tin lid or with aluminium foil to avoid burning.

11. When cooked, remove from the foodi and leave it to stand, in its tin, for between 10 and 20 minutes before turning out onto a wire rack.

12. When cooled, melt some chocolate over the top or drizzle icing all over it. Enjoy

CHOCCY-BANANA CAKE Ⓥ

INGREDIENTS

- 250g of Plain flour
- 220g softened Butter
- 120g of Sugar
- 4 medium-sized Eggs
- 1 ½ teaspoons of Baking powder
- 2 teaspoons of Vanilla essence
- 4 tablespoons of Whole milk
- 4 Bananas
- A handful of chocolate drops

Serves	4-5
Difficulty	●○○
Functions	Bake/Roast
Time Prep	5
Time Cook	40

METHOD

1. Insert the steaming rack into the cooking pot with the horizontal part closer to the bottom. Pre-heat the cooking pot by selecting BAKE/ROAST for 3 minutes at 150°C. Peel and mash the bananas. Combine all the ingredients in a large mixing bowl.

2. Grease a cake tin with margarine and dust with flour. Add the mixture into the cake tin and carefully place into

the cooking pot. Select BAKE/ROAST and bake for 40 minutes at 150°C. Remove the tin and allow to cool. Enjoy.

VICTORIA SPONGE CAKE ⓥ

INGREDIENTS

- Strawberry jam
- 150g of Sugar
- A glug of Whole milk
- 2 large/3 small Eggs
- 1 teaspoon of Baking powder
- 1 teaspoon of Vanilla essence
- 150g of Self-raising flour
- 150g of Margarine or softened butter
- Buttercream or fresh cream for the sponge filling
- Icing sugar for dusting the top

Serves	4-6
Difficulty	●●○
Functions	**Bake/Roast**
Time Prep	**5**
Time Cook	**35+**

METHOD

1. In a large mixing bowl, add the margarine and the sugar, mix well into a cream paste. Add a teaspoon of vanilla essence and continue to mix. Crack one egg into the bowl and mix it in well.

2. Over the bowl add the flour into a sieve and add the baking powder to the flour, shaking a little through before adding another egg, then more flour and so on until all the flour and egg is folded in well to the mixture.

3. After the mixture is fully combined, use a spoon to lift out some of the mixture. If it drops from the spoon back into the bowl, then the consistency is fine. If the mixture sticks to the spoon, then a dash of milk is needed. Repeat the drop test and keep adding a little milk until the consistency is reached.

4. Grease a cake tin (that fits in the Foodi cooking pot) with margarine. Leave no part not greased. Add a handful of flour to the tin and shake it around to dust it. This ensures that the mixture does not stick to the sides. Add the mixture and if the tin is small, use a knife to level it at the top.

5. Put the cake tin into the Foodi cooking pot. Select BAKE/ROAST and cook for 55 minutes at 160°C. Check the cake at 50 minutes. If it is burning, cover in greaseproof paper or aluminium foil. Remove the tin from the Foodi carefully and leave to cool. After 20 minutes, remove from the tin and leave on a wire rack.

6. Fill with buttercream, jam or both. Enjoy.

7. Note for small tins, this should be enough for both halves of the cake, for large tins, make it twice!

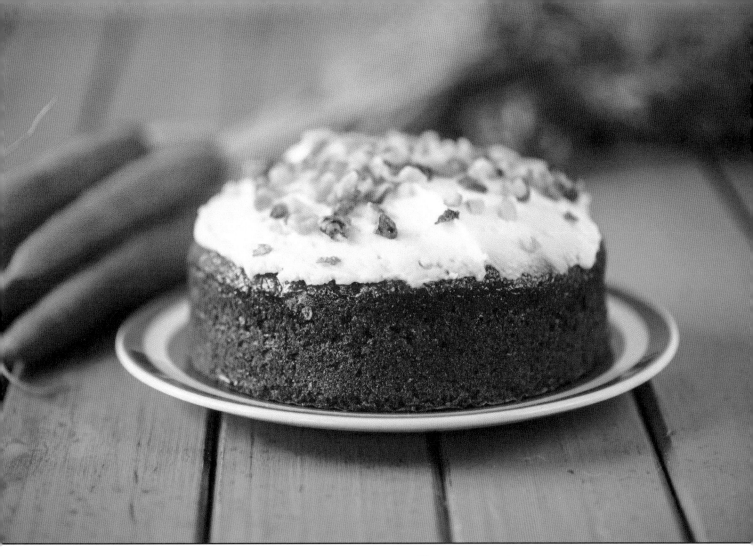

SOFT & MOIST CARROT CAKE ⓥ

INGREDIENTS FOR THE CAKE

- 170ml Sunflower oil
- 170g Caster sugar
- 3 medium-sized Eggs
- 50g Chopped walnuts

Serves	6
Difficulty	●○○
Functions	**Bake/Roast**
Time Prep	5
Time Cook	25+

- 90g of grated Carrots
- 170g Plain flour
- 20g of Oatmeal
- 1 teaspoon of Vanilla essence
- 1 teaspoon of Bicarbonate of soda
- 1 teaspoon of ground Cinnamon
- 1 teaspoon of Baking powder

- 85g of Soft cheese (such as full-fat Philadelphia, not the reduced fat version)
- 60g of Butter
- ½ a teaspoon of Vanilla essence
- 115g of Icing sugar

Method

1. Peel the carrots. Crack the eggs into a bowl and beat with a fork.

2. Take a large mixing bowl and grate the carrots into it. Add the sunflower oil, caster sugar, the eggs, the chopped walnuts, the flour (through a sieve), the oatmeal, a teaspoon of vanilla essence, a teaspoon of bicarinate of soda, a teaspoon of ground cinnamon and a teaspoon of baking powder.

3. Mix really thoroughly, either by hand or with the help of a mixer.

4. Open the lid of the Foodi and place the steaming rack into it with the horizontal shelf closest to the bottom of the cooking pot.

5. Grease the inside of a cake tin that fits into the cooking pot with some butter or margarine then dust lightly with some flour.

6. Tip the mixture from the mixing bowl into the cake tin and put it into the cooking pot on top of the steaming rack. Close the lid.

7. Select BAKE/ROAST. Bake the cake for 21 minutes at 160°C.

8. Open the Foodi lid and add a metal lid to the cake tin or cover it with foil to avoid burning.

9. Remove the steaming rack. Select BAKE/ROAST and bake for 15 minutes at 180°C.

10. During the last 5 minutes of the baking time, check the consistency of the cake with a toothpick to see if it is too gooey or firm. If firm enough, press the stop button to end cooking. Add more time if not quite done.

11. Cooking time varies depending on the width of the cake tin and therefore the height of the cake being baked. For reference, I use a 20cm diameter round cake tin with a loose-fitting base.

12. For the topping, take a mixing bowl and add the soft cheese, the butter, half a teaspoon of vanilla essence and the icing sugar. Beat well using a fork. Remove the cake from the cooking pot and allow to cool.

13. After 20 minutes, either push up the loose-fitting base to remove the sides of the tin or flip out onto a wire cooling tray by placing the wire tray on top of the tin and flipping 180°, slowly easing up the cake tin until it is cleanly removed.

14. When cool enough to apply the topping, use a soft plastic or silicone spatula to evenly spread the topping cream all over the top of the cake.

15. If you wish to have not just the top of the cake creamed, simply double the topping ingredients and this yields enough to cover the sides of the cake too. For decoration, I like to add a few walnut halves on the top.

16. Wait for the cake to be completely cool before slicing the cake and enjoying it.

HILARY'S MELT-IN-YOUR-MOUTH FRUIT SCONES ⓥ

Figure 8: Double the ingredients used in this recipe yielded 11 scones, six in the first batch and five in the second batch. My Father scored them 10/10.

INGREDIENTS

- 225g of self-raising flour
- 50g of Sultanas
- 150ml of Whole milk
- 1 Egg
- 30g of Sugar
- 60g of Butter
- ½ a teaspoon of Salt

Serves	6
Difficulty	●●○
Functions	**Bake/Roast**
Time Prep	**10**
Time Cook	**15**

METHOD

1. You will need a biscuit cutter for this recipe. For the timing in this recipe, a 7cm wide biscuit cutter was used.

2. Crack and beat the egg in a small cup. Take a large mixing bowl and sift the flour and the salt into it using a sieve. Add the sultanas. Chop the butter into small cubes and rub it into the flour using just your fingertips. The resultant mixture should resemble breadcrumbs. Add the sugar and mix it in well.

3. Make a well in the centre of the bowl and pour in the milk, stirring very well, always taking the flour from the edge of the bowl with a spoon.

4. With some more flour, sprinkle a little to dust your work surface, pick up the dough and knead it until it is smooth. Shape the dough into a 2 ½ cm thick flat lump on the surface. Dust the edges of the biscuit cutter in flour and press firmly into the dough. Repeat until no more complete forms can be cut. Then reshape the dough and repeat until all of the dough is now in equally-sized scones. Brush the tops of each scone with beaten egg.

5. Open the lid of the Foodi and place the air crisp basket into the cooking pot. Select BAKE/ROAST and cook at 170°C for 2 minutes to pre-heat the device.

6. Grease the basket lightly with margarine or butter. Fit the scones into the basket and close the lid.

7. Select BAKE/ROAST and cook for 12-13 minutes at 170°C, checking in the last minute that they are not too brown.

8. Remove from the air crisp basket and allow to cool on a wire rack. When cool, slice in half and either spread with butter, cream, strawberry jam or any combination of those classic accomplices!

GRILLED ORANGES WITH CINNAMON-SUGAR & GRANOLA ⓥ

INGREDIENTS

- 2 large Oranges
- ½ a tablespoon of ground cinnamon
- ½ a tablespoon of Demerera sugar
- Granola oats to decorate (optional)
- Fresh mint to decorate (optional)
- Strawberries to decorate (optional)
- Cashew nuts to decorate (optional)

Serves	2-4
Difficulty	ooo
Functions	**Grill**
Time Prep	2
Time Cook	5

METHOD

9. Put the steaming rack into the cooking por of the Foodi with its horizontal rack at the lowest position. Pre-heat the Foodi by selecting GRILL for 4 minutes and carry on with the preparation.

10. Cut each orange in half across the centre, so that one half of each orange has the stalk end in the centre. Use a knife or the handle-end of a teaspoon to remove any seeds from the exposed centres of the orange halves.

11. Using a shape knife, loosen the segment halves of the oranges so that they can come away from the orange peel easily after cooking.

12. In a small bowl mix the cinnamon and the sugar well. With each orange half facing flat-side upwards, carefully spoon half a teaspoon of the sugar-cinnamon mix across the top. Use the back of the spoon then to evenly distribute the sugar.

13. Carefully place the orange halves onto the steaming rack with their sugar-coated side facing upwards.

14. Close the lid and select GRILL and grill them for 5 minutes. Check in the last minute that they are not burning. If the sugar has not "melted" or caramelized after the 5 minutes is up, grill for a further minute or so. It should be golden brown and bubbles should be forming at the top.

15. Serve each orange half on a plate. Sprinkle half a handful of granola on the top of each orange half and add a mint leaf as decoration. Eat with a tea spoon.

SOUP RECIPES

The Ninja Foodi is the ideal kitchen gadget for making soups. It has a large pot, can pressure cook if needs must and heats from all directions. Compared to a standard large saucepan, the Foodi will be able to cook a soup in just the fraction of the normal time.

Some of these recipes require that you have a hand blender to mix up the chunky ingredients into a cream-like liquid.

PEA & MINT SOUP

BUTTERNUT SQUASH SOUP Ⓥ

INGREDIENTS

- 1 large Butternut squash
- 1 Green apple
- 1 Garlic clove
- 2 large Carrots
- 1 Onion
- 1 litre of Boiling water
- 80ml Cream
- 2 Vegetable stock cubes or 2 vegetable OXO cubes
- Olive oil
- Salt
- Pepper
- Ground cinnamon
- Ground nutmeg

Serves	4-6
Difficulty	●●○
Functions	**Sear/Sauté Pressure**
Time Prep	**7**
Time Cook	**25**

METHOD

1. Chop the butternut squash into 1cm cubes. Peel and dice the onion

2. Peel and core the apple. Peel and slice the carrot into thin slices

3. Open the Foodi lid, remove accessories and add a tablespoon of olive oil

4. Select SEAR/SAUTÉ on the high setting

5. When the oil has warmed, add the diced onion. Cook for 1 minute

6. Press the garlic clove into the pot. Cook both ingredients until the onions have become glassy.

7. Dice the apple and add it to the pot.

8. Add the butternut squash cubes, carrot slices and 1 litre of boiling water. Crumble in the vegetable stock cubes. Stir well.

9. Install the pressure lid, switch the vent to SEAL. Select PRESSURE. Pressure cook on the high setting for 12 minutes.

10. After the countdown timer has reached zero, switch the vent to VENT and quickly release the pressure. Remove the pressure lid, add the cream and season with salt, pepper, two large pinches of cinnamon and nutmeg. Stir well.

11. Transfer large amounts of the soup to the measuring jug, never more than half of the jug full at a time. Use a hand-blender to reduce the soup to a cream-like consistency.

12. After blending, pour into a large saucepan and repeat until all of the soup in the cooking pot has been blended.

HEARTY TOMATO SOUP Ⓥ

INGREDIENTS

- 9 tomatoes
- 1 Red onion
- 3 Garlic cloves
- 1 tablespoon of Balsamic vinegar
- ½ teaspoon Salt

Serves	4-5
Difficulty	●●○
Functions	**Bake/Roast Pressure**
Time Prep	5
Time Cook	25

- ½ teaspoon Sugar
- ½ teaspoon Black pepper
- 1 tablespoon Olive oil
- 2 tablespoon Tomato puree
- 1 tablespoon Brown sugar
- 1 tablespoon dried Basil
- Fresh basil leaves (optional)
- 2 Chicken stock cubes
- 700ml water

METHOD

1. Quarter the tomatoes and dice the onion

2. Open the Foodi lid, remove the accessories and put the tomatoes and onion in,

3. Crush the garlic. Add the garlic, balsamic vinegar, salt and pepper.

4. Drizzle olive oil over the ingredients. Select BAKE/ROAST for 10 minutes at 200°C.

5. When done, add the tomato puree, brown sugar, dried basil, the chicken stock cubes (crumbled), sugar and 700ml water

6. Fit the pressure lid and switch the vent dial to SEAL. Select PRESSURE. Pressure cook for 5 minutes on high

7. When the countdown timer has reached zero, allow the timer to count up to 5 minutes as a natural release. Remove the pressure lid.

8. Transfer large amounts of the soup to the measuring jug, never more than half of the jug full at a time.

9. Use a hand-blender to reduce the soup to a cream-like consistency.

10. After blending, pour into a large saucepan and repeat until all of the soup in the cooking pot has been blended.

11. Add a little cream using a spoon to the center if you wish.

VEGAN LENTIL SOUP ⓥ

INGREDIENTS

- 2 large Onions
- 3 large Carrots
- 1 Tomato
- ¼ of a Turnip or swede
- 100g red lentils
- 4 Vegetable stock cubes or vegetable OXO cubes

- 1 litre of boiling water
- Olive oil
- Salt
- Pepper
- Parsley (optional for decoration)
- Lemon (optional for decoration)

Serves	4
Difficulty	●●○
Functions	Sear/Sauté Pressure
Time Prep	5
Time Cook	35

METHOD

1. Peel and dice the onions. Cube the tomato.

2. Peel and chop the carrots and turnip into thin slices

3. Boil the kettle and pour 1 litre of water into a measuring jug. Dissolve the stock cubes into the water and mix well.

4. Remove accessories from the cooking pot. Add a dessert spoon of olive oil to the pot and select SEAR/SAUTÉ, use the high setting.

5. Add the diced onion and stir well

6. After 4 minutes add the carrots, tomato and turnip

7. Stir and sauté for around 3 minutes

8. Add the vegetable stock and continue to cook for 5 minutes. Add the lentils. Stir well and leave to bubble away for 5 minutes. Add salt and pepper.

9. Fit the pressure lid, switch the vent to SEAL and select PRESSURE. Cook for 15 minutes.

10. Switch the vent dial to VENT to release the pressure.

11. Optional: Transfer large amounts of the soup to the measuring jug, never more than half of the jug full at a time. Use a hand-blender to reduce the soup to a cream-like consistency. After blending, pour into a large saucepan and repeat until all of the soup in the cooking pot has been blended.

12. Serve and garnish with a quarter of the lemon on the side of the bowl and sprinkle some crushed pistachio nuts in the centre.

LEEK AND POTATO SOUP Ⓥ

INGREDIENTS

- 4 Potatoes
- 4 Medium sized leeks or 3 large leeks
- 1 Large onion
- 1 tablespoon of unsalted butter
- 250ml Skimmed milk
- 1 Vegetable stock cube
- 850ml boiling water
- Salt & Pepper to season
- Croutons to garnish (optional)

Serves	4+
Difficulty	●●○
Functions	Sear/Sauté Pressure
Time Prep	7
Time Cook	25

METHOD

1. Peel and dice the onion. Peel and dice the potatoes into bite-sized cubes. Slice the leeks along the length and pull apart. Wash the sheets of leek under cold water to remove residual mud from between the layers. Stack the leek layers and slice through them into 1cm wide pieces

2. Boil 850ml of water and in a measuring jug, add a vegetable stock cube OR vegetable OXO cube. Turn on the Foodi and remove accessories from the cooking pot. Select the SEAR/SAUTÉ function and start it on the high setting in order to pre-heat. Add a large knob of butter and let it melt.

3. Throw in the diced onion and leek and allow them to fry slightly in the butter. They should not get brown at this stage. Add the potatoes as soon as the aroma of the leek and onion is noticeable.

4. Turn off the Foodi and back on again. This time select SEAR/SAUTÉ and use the low setting. Put the pressure lid onto the device and make sure the vent is set to VENT. Sauté the ingredients for 8 minutes on the low setting. Remove the lid and add the milk and the stock from the measuring jug. Add a good pinch of both salt and pepper. Stir well. Return the pressure lid to the Foodi, this time with the vent switched to SEAL.

5. Select PRESSURE and cook on the high setting for 6 minutes. Switch the vent to VENT and allow the pressure to release. Stir well after removing the lid.

6. Transfer large amounts of the soup to the measuring jug, never more than half of the jug full at a time. Use a hand-blender to reduce the soup to a cream-like consistency. After blending, pour into a large saucepan and repeat until all of the soup in the cooking pot has been blended.

Tips

Add one pressed garlic clove in stage 9 if you wish to have a stronger flavour.

For much creamier soup, use whole milk or use less milk and add cream.

SWEET POTATO & ONION SOUP ⓥ

INGREDIENTS

- 1 Carrot
- 2 Onions
- 2 Garlic cloves
- 300ml Orange juice
- 600ml of boiling Water
- 900g of Sweet potatoes
- 1 Vegetable stock cube or 1 vegetable OXO cube
- 225ml of low-fat Yoghurt
- A few sprigs of fresh Coriander
- 2 tablespoons of Olive oil
- Salt & Pepper to season
- Orange peel (optional as garnish)
- More fresh Coriander (optional as garnish)

Serves	4
Difficulty	●○○
Functions	**Sear/Sauté Pressure**
Time Prep	**15**
Time Cook	**35**

METHOD

1. Boil a kettle of water with at least 650ml of water in it. Peel and dice the sweet potatoes into 1 cm cubes. Peel and dice the carrot. Peel and slice the onions into thin slices. Peel the garlic cloves. Chop the fresh coriander well. In a measuring jug, pour 600ml of boiling water from the kettle and dissolve the vegetable stock cube into it.

2. Remove accessories from the cooking pot and add 2 tablespoons of olive oil to it. Select SEAR/SAUTE using the medium temperature setting. Add the onion, carrot, sweet potato to the pot. Crush the garlic cloves into the pot. Stir regularly to sauté the vegetables for 6 to 7 minutes until they start to soften.

3. Pour in the prepared vegetable stock and the orange juice. Cook for a few minutes until everything is bubbling away nicely.

4. Install the pressure lid and switch the vent dial to SEAL. Pressure cook the contents for 8 minutes using the high setting. It will take a while to reach pressure. After the countdown timer reaches zero, allow the pressure to release naturally for 5 minutes before switching the vent dial to VENT. Allow the pressure to quick release, quickly closing it if any liquid spurts from the vent. Stir well after removing the lid.

5. Transfer large amounts of the soup to the measuring jug, never more than half of the jug full at a time. Use a hand-blender to reduce the soup to a cream-like consistency. After blending, pour into a large saucepan and repeat until all of the soup in the cooking pot has been blended.

6. Stir in the yoghurt and chopped coriander. Season to taste with salt and pepper. Serve the soup with a ladle into deep plates or soup bowls. Garnish with fresh coriander on top of orange rind. Enjoy

THAI COCONUT SOUP

INGREDIENTS

- 1 Red chili
- 250ml Coconut milk
- 1 Lemongrass
- 1 Spring onion
- 1 Lime
- 1 teaspoon of Chicken stock (1 chicken stock cube)
- 100g Button mushrooms
- 20g of Fresh ginger (about the size of a thumb)
- 2 Chicken breast fillets
- Olive oil
- Salt & Pepper

Serves	2-3
Difficulty	●●○
Functions	Sear/Sauté
Time Prep	5
Time Cook	25

METHOD

1. Boil a kettle. In a measuring jug, add 250ml of boiling water and the chicken stock. Stir well to mix

2. Cut the chicken breast fillets into mouth-sized chunks. Wash the lime. Grate the zest of the lime into a small bowl for later.

3. Cut the lime in half. Cut the chili lengthways and remove the seeds. Cut each chili half into small strips. Peel and grate the ginger into another small bowl.

4. Cut the mushrooms into quarters. With the aid of a flat kitchen knife, press the flat of the knife hard down onto the lemongrass to start the release of the aromatic oils contained within. Bend in half or cut in half along the short width and not lengthways.

5. Remove the roots from the spring onion and slice into fine rings, keeping the green and white parts of the onion separate from one another. The green parts will be used later for decoration.

6. Open the Foodi and remove all accessories. Add a dessert spoon of olive oil and select SEAR/SAUTÉ and start to heat up the oil. When the oil is hot, add the chicken breast chunks, the ginger, the lemon grass, mushrooms and the white parts of the spring onion. Cook for 3 minutes, stirring well

7. Select the medium temperature setting. Add the prepared chicken stock and the coconut milk. Stir in well. Cook on the medium heat for 5 minutes. If you have a frying pan lid, put it on the top of the Foodi to keep some of the liquid in. Remove the lemongrass and add the chili strips, the lime zest, the juice of the lime, season with salt and pepper as required.

8. Use a large plastic ladle to dish out the soup into two or three soup bowls.

9. Decorate with the green parts of the spring onion. Enjoy

HEARTY POTATO SOUP

1. Boil a kettle with around 500ml of water in it. Remove any accessories from the Foodi. Peel the sweet potato, the potatoes and the carrots. Slice the potatoes into 1cm cubes and the carrot into 1/2cm cubes. Remove the bottom 1cm of the leek and cut lengthways. Stack the leek leaves and wash thoroughly under a tap. Slice the leek into 1cm wide slices. Slice the celery into ½ cm thick half-moon shapes. Peel and halve the onion and chop into fine strips. Take a measuring jug and add 400ml of boiling water. Add the chicken stock and stir until dissolved.

INGREDIENTS

- 1 small Sweet potato
- 1 Celery stick
- 1 Leek
- 1 Carrot
- 1 Onion
- A handful of Fresh chives
- 2 large Potatoes
- 1 teaspoon of Chicken stock / 1 chicken stock cube or a chicken OXO cube
- 80g Bacon lardons / Pancetta lardons
- 4 Hot dog sausages (packet or jar, drained)
- Salt & Pepper

Serves	2-3
Difficulty	●●○
Functions	Sear/Sauté
Time Prep	5
Time Cook	30

2. Select SEAR/SAUTÉ using the medium setting. Without adding any oil, throw the bacon or pancetta lardons into the cooking pot as well as the chopped onion slices. Use a wooden spoon to stir regularly to avoid sticking. Cook for 2-3 minutes until the onion becomes glassy.

3. Add the celery, carrot, potato, sweet potato, leek and stir for a further 2-3 minutes until you can smell the leek cooking. Add the prepared jug of chicken stock and add a little salt if required.

4. If you have a frying pan lid that may fit the Foodi, put it over the top and let everything cook for 12-15 minutes, until the vegetables are soft. (If you do not have a lid, reduce the temperature to low and let it all cook for 20 minutes, adding more boiled water if there is not enough in the pot).

5. Cut the hot dog sausages into 1cm thick chunks and add them to the pot for the last part of the cooking time above. The sausages will warm through really quickly. Stir well.Cut the chives into 2mm long tubes. Add salt and pepper if required. Serve into 2 or 3 deep plates or bowls.

6. Decorate with the fresh chives. Enjoy

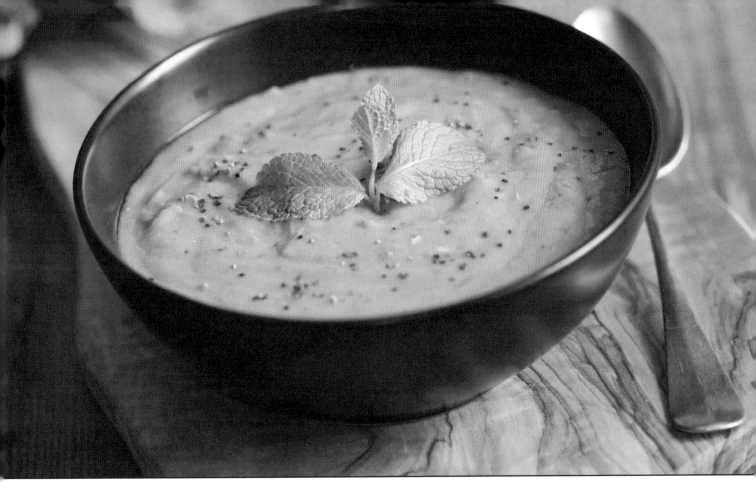

PEA & MINT SOUP Ⓥ

INGREDIENTS

- 500g of frozen Peas
- 1 Onion
- 2 Garlic cloves
- 1 large Potato
- 125ml of Cream
- 2 Vegetable stock cubes of 2 vegetable OXO

Serves	6
Difficulty	●○○
Functions	**Sear/Sauté**
Time Prep	**5**
Time Cook	**25**

cubes (or replace with 1 chicken stock cube)

- A sprig of fresh Mint or 1 tablespoon of dried mint
- 2 tablespoons of Butter
- Salt & Pepper to season

METHOD

1. Boil a kettle of 750ml or more water.

2. Peel and dice the onion.

3. Peel and chop the potatoes into 1cm cubes. Peel the garlic and slice it into wafer thin slices.

4. If using fresh mint, scrunch it together in your hand and chop it finely.

5. Remove accessories from the cooking pot and add the butter into it.

6. Select SEAR/SAUTE using the high setting. When the butter has melted, throw in the potato, the onion and the garlic. Stir well until the potato is lightly browned.

7. Add the peas to the pot and mix through for 2 minutes. Add a generous pinch of salt and add a few twists of cracked pepper.

8. Add 700ml of boiling water and crumble in the stock cubes. Add the cream.

9. When the stock starts boiling, reduce the temperature to the SEAR/SAUTE low setting. Install the pressure lid, switch the vent dial to VENT and let it cook for about 10 minutes.

10. Check near the end of the cooking time, the peas should be very soft but still the same green as when they first went in. Add the mint and stir in well.

11. Get a large saucepan ready and with the aid of a ladle, scoop full ladles of the soup into a measuring jug or similar, the jug should be never more than half full. Use a hand blender to blend the soup into a cream-like consistency.

12. Tip the soup into the saucepan and repeat until all of the contents of the cooking pot have been blended.

13. Heat the saucepan a little until hot enough to serve. If you have any fresh mint, use a few leaves to decorate each bowl of soup. Crack some black pepper over the top and do not mix in. Enjoy.

BEEF AND MACARONI SOUP

INGREDIENTS

- 1kg of Minced beef
- 1 Onion
- 1 – 2 Garlic cloves, depending on size
- 2 cans of finely Chopped tomato or puree
- 8 cocktail or cherry Tomatoes
- 2 tablespoons of Worcestershire sauce
- A regular sized box (500g) of dried Tortiglioni, Rigatoni Penne, or Macaroni pasta
- 1 teaspoon of dried Oregano
- 2 Carrots
- 2 Beef stock cubes or 2 beef OXO cubes
- 1 ½ litres of Boiling water
- 2 Bay leaves
- 1 tablespoon of Olive oil

Serves	6+
Difficulty	●●○
Functions	Sear/Sauté Pressure
Time Prep	10
Time Cook	20

METHOD

1. Peel and dice the onion

2. Peel and slice the carrots into thick chunks.

3. Wash the cocktail or cherry tomatoes, remove the green stalks. Do not slice or chop.

4. Open the Tomato cans

5. Start a kettle boiling with at least 1 ½ litres of water.

6. Open the Foodi lid, remove accessories and add a tablespoon of olive oil

7. Select SEAR/SAUTÉ on the high setting

8. When the oil has warmed, add the diced onion. Cook for 1 minute

9. Press the garlic into the pot and add a good pinch of salt and pepper

10. Cook for a further 1 minute.

11. Add the minced beef. Break up with a wooden spoon and stir well. Cook until the meat is no longer pink.

12. If an abundance of fat is clear at the bottom of the pot, use a sieve to remove as much as possible.

13. Add the chopped carrot chunks, 1 ½ litres of boiling water from the kettle, beef stock cubes crumbled, tomatoes, canned tomatoes, Worcestershire sauce, oregano, bay leaves and the pasta.

14. Mix very well together.

15. Fit the pressure lid, switch the vent to SEAL and select PRESSURE.

16. Pressure-cook the ingredients on the high setting for 5 minutes.

17. After the pressure cooking is complete and the countdown timer has reached zero, switch the vent to VENT and allow the pressure to quick release.

18. Open the lid, stir well and serve.

19. If the soup is too liquid, use the SEAR/SAUTÉ function on the high setting to thicken up the sauce.

Season as desired with salt and pepper.

CREAMY COURGETTE SOUP WITH PANCETTA

INGREDIENTS

- 2 large courgettes
- 4 Medium-sized potatoes
- 2 Onions
- 160g of Bacon lardons or pancetta
- 1 Baguette
- 2 Garlic cloves
- 1 teaspoon of ground Nutmeg
- 2 teaspoon of Chicken stock powder or 2 chicken stock cubes
- 400ml of cream (double cream to make it extra creamy)
- Salt & Pepper
- Olive oil

Serves	4-6
Difficulty	●○○
Functions	Sear/Sauté Pressure
Time Prep	5
Time Cook	20

METHOD

1. Peel the potatoes and cut into 2cm small cubes. Remove the ends off the courgette and cut into 2cm cubes.

2. Boil a kettle with at least 850ml of water in it.

3. Peel the garlic clove and chop finely with a sharp knife. Peel the onion and dice into small cubes.

4. Remove accessories from the cooking pot and select SEAR/SAUTE using the high temperature setting.

5. When the pot is hot, add the pancetta or bacon lardons. Stir to avoid sticking as they should crisp up nicely without the need for added oil.

6. When they have crisped, carefully remove the cooking pot and tip out the lardons into a bowl for use later. Add the pot back into the Foodi without emptying the bacon fat from it.

7. Again, using the SEAR/SAUTE function with the high temperature setting, add the potatoes, the courgette and the onion cubes. Stir them well for 3 minutes.

8. Add 800ml of boiling water and the chicken stock. Stir until dissolved.

9. Warm up an oven to 200°C. Slice the baguette into 4 equally long pieces, cutting each in half.

10. Add the baguette to the oven cut-side facing upwards and let it warm through for 5 minutes. Remove when it's done but continue with the recipe as it warms through

11. Fit the pressure lid and turn the vent dial to SEAL. Select PRESSURE and cook at the high setting for 5 minutes. It will take a long time to reach pressure due to the amount of liquid in the pot.

12. After the timer counter has reached zero, carefully switch the vent dial to VENT to release the pressure quickly. If liquid spurts from the vent, immediately return the dial to SEAL, wait a few minutes and switch again to VENT until the lid can be removed.

13. Carefully drizzle olive oil across the upward-facing cut-side of the baguette slices and liberally scatter the garlic slices into the oiled surface.

14. Return to the oven for a further 3 minutes to toast (use the middle shelf of the oven).

15. Add the cream to the soup. Add the nutmeg and season with salt and pepper. Mix in well.

16. Using a measuring jug, remove ladles full of the soup and blend using a hand blender.

17. Pour the soup liquid into a saucepan, add more ladles and repeat until all of the soup has been blended into a pleasant, green creamy liquid.

18. Divide the soup into soup bowls. If you have any cream left-over, drizzle a spoonful or two over the top of the soup, swirling it gently into the soup for decoration.

19. Sprinkle bacon lardons carefully so that they sit on the surface of the soup. Serve with garlic baguette and enjoy.

CONVERSION TABLES

SIMPLIFIED OVEN TEMPERATURES

Fahrenheit °F	Celsius °C	Gas Mark	Description
225	105	1/3	very cool
250	120	1/2	
275	130	1	cool
300	150	2	
325	165	3	very moderate
350	180	4	moderate
375	190	5	
400	200	6	moderately hot
425	220	7	hot
450	230	8	
475	245	9	very hot

SIMPLIFIED LIQUID MEASURES

ml	Fl oz/pint	Pint	Litre
25 ml	1 fl oz	3 pints	1.7 litre
50 ml	2 fl oz	3 ¼ pint	1.8 litre
150 ml	5 fl oz ¼ pint	3 ½ pint	2 litre
200 ml	7 fl oz ⅓ pint	3 ¾ pint	2.1 litre
300 ml	10 fl oz ½ pint	4 pint	2.3 litre
450ml	15 fl oz ¾ pint	4 ¼ pint	2.4 litre
500+ ml	20 fl oz 1 pint	4 ½ pint	2.6 litre
568 ml	1 pint	4 ¾ pint	2.7 litre
750 ml	1 ¼ pint	5 pint	2.8 litre
900 ml	1 ½ pint	5 ¼ pint	3 litre
1 litre	1 ¾ pint	5 ½ pint	3.1 litre
1.1 litre	2 pint	5 ¾ pint	3.3 litre
1.3 litre	2 ¼ pint	6 pint	3.4 litre
1.4 litre	2 ½ pint	6 ¼ pint	3.5 litre
1.6 litre	2 ¾ pint	6 ½ pint	3.7 litre

SIMPLIFIED OUNCES TO GRAMS CHART

Ounces	Grams
1/2 oz	15g
1 oz	30g
2 oz	60g
3 oz	90g
4 oz	110g
5 oz	140g
6 oz	170g
7 oz	200g
8 oz	225g
9 oz	255g
10 oz	280g
11 oz	310g
12 oz	340g
13 oz	370g
14 oz	400g
15 oz	425g
1 lb	453g
2 lb	907g

UK pint = 20 fl oz

US pint = 16 fl oz

SIMPLIFIED MILLILITRES TO AMERICAN SPOONS

ml	teaspoon	ml	table spoon
1.25 ml	¼ teaspoon	30 ml	2 tablespoons
2.5 ml	½ teaspoon	45 ml	3 tablespoons
5 ml	1 teaspoon	60 ml	4 tablespoons
10 ml	2 teaspoons	75 ml	5 tablespoons
15 ml	1 tablespoon	90 ml	6 tablespoons

SIMPLIFIED AMERICAN SPOON TO AMERICAN CUPS

Spoon	American Cups
1 tablespoon	1/16 Cup
2 tablespoons	1/8 Cup
4 tablespoons	1/4 Cup
5 tablespoons	1/3 Cup
8 tablespoons	1/2 Cup
10 tablespoons	2/3 Cup

ADDITIONAL SAUCES/DIPS & STUFFING

Mentioned in some recipes in this book, it seemed mean not to share the sauces or dips that I recommend pairing the food with, even though they do not require the Foodi to prepare them.

GUACAMOLE DIP

AIOLI DIP ⓥ

INGREDIENTS

- 4 Garlic cloves
- 300ml of good Olive oil
- 3 Egg yolks
- 2 tablespoons of Lemon juice
- 1 tablespoon of Panko breadcrumbs
- Sea salt & Pepper to season

Serves	6
Difficulty	●●●
Functions	-
Time Prep	15
Time Cook	0

METHOD

1. Chop the garlic very fine with a sharp knife or a smooth grater. Add sea salt to the garlic slices and use the flat edge of the kitchen knife to smooth the garlic and salt into a paste that will eventually become smooth in texture.

2. Move the garlic paste into a measuring jug and add just the yolks of the eggs to it (carefully crack each egg into two halves and cup the content back and forth, allowing the white to drip away but keeping the yellow yolk in the shell halves).

3. Use a hand blender or a mixer to cream the garlic into the egg yolk. Use a silicone spatula to ensure that the egg around the wall of the jug is used again and mixed with the garlic. Slowly stir the mix with the spatula while adding the olive oil, folding it in with the egg. This takes a while to blend in per hand but eventually you will have a mayonnaise.

4. Add a tablespoon of lemon juice and breadcrumbs. Use the hand mixer again to combine well. Add sea salt and pepper. Don't be afraid to add more lemon juice if necessary. Transfer the dip to as many ramekins as needed, use the silicone spatula to get every drop out of the jug.

SUPER SPICY MAYONNAISE DIP ⓥ

INGREDIENTS

- 240ml of Mayonnaise
- 1 Garlic clove
- 3 tablespoons of Sriracha sauce
- The juice from ½ a lemon or 2 tablespoons

Serves	6
Difficulty	●○○
Functions	-
Time Prep	5
Time Cook	0

METHOD

1. Peel, then crush the garlic clove into a bowl. Add all the other ingredients. Mix well together with a whisk.

GUACAMOLE DIP ⓥ

INGREDIENTS

- 175g ripened Avocado
- 1 tablespoon of Lemon juice
- 2 Tomatoes
- 1 Lemon
- 100g of low-fat Soft cheese (such as Philadelphia, even better is the herbal version)
- 4 Spring onions
- Tobasco sauce
- Salt & Pepper to season
- Chives (to garnish)

Serves	6
Difficulty	●○○
Functions	-
Time Prep	5
Time Cook	0

METHOD

1. Remove the roots of the spring onions and finely chop them.

2. Chop the tomatoes, discarding the stalks first.

3. Mash the avocado innards with the lemon juice in a bowl. Add the spring onions, a few drops of the tobasco sauce, the tomatoes, the zest of the lemon (use a grater to grate the skin, go all around the lemon), the soft cheese, salt and pepper.

4. Mix well and serve with crispy potato skins from the beginning of this book.

SAGE & ONION STUFFING ⓥ

INGREDIENTS

- 150g of Butter
- Salt & Pepper
- 1 large Onion
- 1 tablespoon of dried Sage
- 250g of Panko breadcrumbs
- 1 tablespoon of dried Thyme
- 4 tablespoons of dried Parsley

Serves	**4**
Difficulty	●○○
Functions	**Sear/Sauté**
Time Prep	**2**
Time Cook	**24**

METHOD

1. Peel and finely dice the onion. Alternatively, using a food processor to chop very finely. If using fresh herbs, wash, pluck and chop them finely.

2. Remove accessories from the cooking pot and add the butter. Select SEAR/SAUTE and use the medium-high heat setting.

3. Add the diced onion and use a wooden spoon to swish it around in the butter. Cook for around 4 to 5 minutes until it is looking glassy and is very aromatic, do not let it brown. Turn off the Foodi.

4. Slowly introduce the thyme, sage and the breadcrumbs to the onion and butter while stirring slowly. Add salt and pepper and parsley. Mix thoroughly. Form into plum-sized balls using an oiled ice-cream scoop but be careful, everything is pretty hot in there. Rest on some grease-proof paper in the base of the Foodi.

5. Close the built-in lid and select BAKE/ROAST. Cook at 160°C for 18 minutes, checking that the stuffing has not burnt. Transfer into a bowl for use later in your roast dinner preparation.

6. Serve with chicken or turkey.

INDEX OF INGREDIENTS

Quite possibly, this section of the book will not be something that you find useful. Personally, when I scan through a recipe book, I often look at the recipes, check the ingredients and move on. Only later do I ponder to myself, "what was that recipe with the chickpeas?" or "I've got chicken in the fridge that needs using, what was that recipe with the chicken and peanut butter?". So, if you're like me, you might find this section useful!

Not included in this section are ingredients that everyone already has in the cupboard such as salt, pepper and olive oil.